JAGUAR
E TYPE

Osprey AutoHistory

JAGUAR E TYPE
3.8 & 4.2 6-cylinder; 5.3 V12

DENIS JENKINSON

First published in 1982 by Osprey Publishing Limited
27A Floral Street, London WC2E 9DP
Member company of the George Philip Group
First reprint winter 1982
Second reprint spring 1985
Third reprint spring 1986
Fourth reprint early 1987
Fifth reprint spring 1988

United States distribution by

Osceola, Wisconsin 54020, USA

British Library Cataloguing in Publication Data

Jenkinson, Denis
    Jaguar E-type: 3.8 & 4.2 6 cylinder,
    5.3 V12
    1. Jaguar automobile—History
    I. Title   II. Series
    629.2'222   TL215.J3
ISBN 0-85045-437-9

Editor Tim Parker
Associate Michael Sedgwick
Photography Mirco Decet
Design Fred Price

Filmset and printed in England by
BAS Printers Limited, Over Wallop, Hampshire

Contents

Chapter 1
I had all but forgotten the E type

The products of Sir William Lyons began to fascinate me from a very early age. When his startling SS1 was introduced in 1931 I was a 'car mad' schoolboy and that long bonnet, small coupé body, shallow windscreen, cycle-type wings and ultra low build made the SS1 coupé my 'dream' car. I knew nothing of its underpowered side-valve engine or its vague steering, nor of the impracticability of the bodywork. The look of the thing was what attracted me. By the time the SS100 two-seater was introduced in 1935 I was beginning to grow up and was learning about cars like the Bugatti 57 and 2.9-litre Alfa Romeo. Prices were academic in my world so I did not appreciate the value-for-money that the SS100 represented, in spite of its short-comings. What had been striking good looks to a schoolboy became to look rather vulgar to an engineering student, but even so you could not ignore the performance factor, especially of the later $3\frac{1}{2}$-litre version. By 1939 I had been given a ride in a $3\frac{1}{2}$-litre SS100 and even from the passenger seat you could sense that the driver did not have much control over the front wheels. We never did achieve 100 mph with it, but at 95 mph it was

nearly airborne at the front, presumably due to the wind getting under those long voluptuous front mudguards. The rather rubbery feel between the steering wheel and the steering arms, occasioned by a poor steering box did not help.

This particular friend was doing a bit of racing at the time and had quite a good British racing car, so he was used to high speed and knew how cars should feel and react. The SS100 was merely passing through his hands, in a sort of motor-trade way and he soon parted with it leaving us with a rather bad impression of the SS Jaguar of that time. There was nothing wrong with that particular SS100, for another owner raced it in club events with no trouble, albeit on slow twisty circuits.

Naturally the war years put a stop to all sporting activity, and the Jaguar factory turned over to aircraft production and repair, but they were

The classic Jaguar line of high performance cars started with the SS100. Here's E. H. Jacob winning the 1937 Welsh Rally. The author loved the looks but doubted its controllability

soon back into car manufacture after the war. In 1948 the outstanding XK120 was born. To anyone brought up on old-English perpendicular sports cars the XK120 was a revelation, but I had been more interested in European sports cars such as BMW, Bugatti, Alfa Romeo, Delahaye, Talbot-Darracq and so on, always academically of course, so that price never entered into my evaluations of sports cars. The sleek XK120 roadster was a bit too long and narrow for my way of thinking, but was not a bad attempt by a British factory and obviously owed a lot to Carrozzeria Touring the Italian body-builders who created the 1940 Mille Miglia BMW two-seater. One thing you could not fault was the beautiful new six-cylinder twin overhead camshaft engine, of 3.4 litres capacity, nor could you fault its power output of 160 bhp. It really was an impressive thing to look at, with its polished cambox covers, shining black exhaust manifolds, twin S.U. carb-

The XK120 roadster set a new standard for 'line' in production sports cars. More than 30 years after its introduction it still looks sleek and well balanced in profile

urettors and alloy cylinder head; what is more, it was very smooth running and propelled the XK120 roadster very rapidly. Not as rapidly as the 132 mph achieved by a specially prepared factory car when it was demonstrated on the Jabbeke highway in Belgium in 1949, but none the less the XK120 was good for 125 mph in full production trim.

This was really the beginning and the yardstick for post-war performance cars and Jaguar were to maintain that standard, and indeed set the precedents, for years to come. As late as 1939 a timed speed of 100 mph for a fully equipped road-going sports car was something exceptional, and in the immediate post-war years Jaguar established new standards with the XK120. Unfortunately the

A trio of Jaguars pointing in the right direction, their development in conjunction with the C and D type sports/racing cars led to the E type. From right to left an XK120, an XK140 and an XK150, all in roadster form

When the E type appeared at the London Motor Show at Earls Court in 1961 it was justifiably given pride of place on the Jaguar stand, mounted in all its glory on a turn-table which emphasised that from any angle the smoothly-styled coupé was a striking-looking car. No one will dispute that it was the star of the show

Above *Out on the road the E type coupé was every bit as impressive to look at as it was at the Earls Court Show*

Right *One of the factory road-test cars, loaned to the press, was this left-hand drive 3.8 litre coupé with the slightly optimistic number plate. The perspex covers did diffuse the light from the weak Lucas headlamps*

XK120 fell short in many other quarters, for the steering was very little better than the old SS100s, the gearbox was not a classic with its awfully slow change from first to second, and the drum brakes could soon become non-existent if the full potential of that beautiful twin-cam engine was used. The double wishbone and longitudinal torsion bar front suspension was not at all bad, but the rear axle was primitive, being hung

This factory publicity photo of a 1962 E type roadster shows the view that other motorists became used to seeing in their mirrors. Apart from running illegally without a front number plate the car seems to have lost its right-hand headlamp cover

13

on half-elliptic 'cart' springs. While the bodywork was exceedingly good-looking, with comfortable seats and adequate boot space, the actual driving position was rather old-fashioned and cramped, with the steering wheel almost vertical, as in the old SS100, and very close to the driver's chest. This was at a time when the straight-arm driving position was beginning to become fashionable thanks to Stirling Moss, who had got the idea from Dr. Farina, the Alfa Romeo racing driver.

Over the years the XK120 was improved and altered, and developed into the XK140 and later into the XK150, but at no time did any of the models appeal to me personally. You could never dispute the performance though and the value-

Above *The engine-carrying sub-frame fabricated from a combination of round and square-section tubing bolts to the front bulkhead of the monocoque centre-section. The bonnet hinges at the front on a tubular extension of the engine-carrying sub-frame*

Left *Nine E Type roadsters on the production line. Right and left-hand drive cars following one another, dependent solely on the placing of orders*

The 3.8 litre engine of the E type showing the plenum chamber feeding the three SU carburettors from the very large circular air filter behind the right front wheel

for-money of them all, for they were very cheap in relation to cars like Porsche, Lancia, Alfa Romeo and Mercedes-Benz. I did cast an eye at them occasionally, as rack-and-pinion steering appeared on the XK140 and disc brakes on the XK150 together with the 3.8-litre engine, but the primitive chassis, of box-section steel, and the cart-sprung rear axle always remained a bit old-fashioned. Even the bits aforementioned, of which I approved, were a bit late in arriving, but Jaguar Engineering was founded on a rather conservative note and maintained that tradition throughout, even though the company's styling department was very forward thinking.

In 1961 the editor of *Motor Sport* came back from a visit to the Jaguar factory in Browns Lane,

The heart of the E type Jaguar. The brilliant 4.2 litre (this one) XK engine with twin overhead camshafts chain-driven from the front of the crankshaft, the alloy cylinder head fed by three large SU carburettors

Coventry, and said 'I have just seen the car I think you will want'. It was the brand new E type coupé that was about to be shown to the world at the Geneva Motor Show. The following year he arrived at the Monaco Grand Prix in an E type roadster (9699RW) which he had on test, and I borrowed it for a run along the Cote d'Azur and up into the Alpes Maritimes. It was running on the high compression ratio of 9:1 which was quite unsuited to French petrol at the time. Consequently it pinked its head off, which did not endear it to me, but it certainly felt good and the performance was phenomenal. Compared with the Porsche I was running at the time the seats felt awful, with too little support to the back, negligible sideways support and no support at all

A Series One E type roadster with the top folded down presents a strong challenge to the girl model for charm and elegance

The E type in roadster form or coupé form, was a photographers delight and looked impressive no matter where it was posed, as this Series One coupé illustrates

under the knees. I could not imagine sitting in the driving seat for 12 hours on end, as I was in the habit of doing in my travels around Europe. It still had the horrid old Jaguar gearbox, which I could not stand in the XK120, with its slow change from first to second, and no synchromesh on bottom gear. There was no question of snicking into first gear quickly when you arrived at a tight hairpin in the mountains unexpectedly. The headlights were abysmal, what light there was generated by Joseph Lucas (the Prince of Darkness, as rude Americans call him) was well diffused before it got through the headlamp covers which smoothed off the front end so beautifully. It was a super looking car and its affinity to the racing D type Jaguar was something that every racing enthusiast just had to enthuse over. Underneath it was pure D type in its conception, with the central monocoque, space frame to contain the engine at the front, and the added bonus of the very interesting and effective independent rear suspension with inboard brakes. The brakes were disc all round, and well up to the performance of the car.

Undoubtedly the Jaguar firm had taken a big step forward with the E type, and it personified the adage 'racing improves the breed'. Performance was obviously the keynote of this exciting new car and the firm made quite sure that the two weekly motoring magazines, *Autocar* and *Motor*, achieved timed speeds of 150 mph. To offer a fully equipped touring-sports car, as distinct from a racing-sports car, that would do 150 mph with acceleration to match and a fuel consumption of around 18 mpg all for £2000 was really a manu-facturing landmark, and something that no-one else had done. Just as the XK120 took the market by storm, so did the E type. But it was not for me, at least not for the job I was doing of travelling all over Europe without many stops.

The central instrument grouping on the Series One cars in which the dials and switches were mounted on an aluminium background. A separate ignition key and starter button was used and many owners preferred the toggle switches to the later tumbler type for they were very positively either 'on' or 'off'. In the centre is the three position lamps switch

After its initial introduction and the performance image enhanced by the road-test figures, the world at large accepted the E type as King of the Road, and the public came to think of Jaguar and the E type as representing 150 mph and speed with safety. These were the happy days of the 'swinging sixties' when it was not considered immoral to do 150 mph, or to cruise all day at 125 mph, nor was it illegal. With the ability to reach 100 mph in 16 seconds away from the traffic lights, everyone enjoyed the E type, and accepted it as part of the British way of life in those days. Naturally it went down well in the USA, even though the American specification had a choice of lower axle ratios which ultimately limited the

Above *Some E types of 1962/63 vintage featured three windscreen wipers. Here's a factory car 'demonstrating' them in that winter's heavy snow*

Left *The impressive main dials on a 3.8 litre Series One car (still ticking over at 600 rpm!) showing the 160 mph speedometer. The road-test 3.8 litre cars could push the needle nearly to the end of the dial*

Above *The engine of a 3.8 litre Series One car showing the troublesome header-tank which tended to rust through, on the front of the engine*

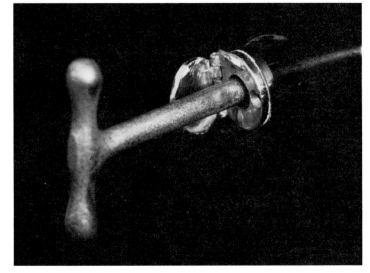

Right *Early cars needed this T-shaped carriage key to unlock the engine cover. It was soon replaced by permanent handles in the cockpit operating rods that passed through the bulkhead*

maximum speed to a bare 120 mph. Its reception in the USA kept the Jaguar order books full to overflowing.

Jaguar agents, like John Coombs of Guildford, soon had E types for competition work and on the first racing appearance in 1961, only weeks after its announcement, Graham Hill won the 25 lap GT Trophy race at Oulton Park in an E type roadster (ECD 400), from an Aston Martin DB4GT while Roy Salvadori was third in another E type roadster (BUY 1). Enthusiasm for racing the E type soon led to the factory experimental department's supplying competition equipment to selected drivers, and ultimately led to a limited run of special Lightweight E types which upheld admirably the Jaguar name in GT racing.

When the E type began to get out into ordinary customer hands few people were dissatisfied with the performance, for in all honesty few customers were capable of driving at 150 mph, and soon backed off when they reached 130 mph and found the car still accelerating impressively. Some of the racing fraternity had E types and found that the normal production model began to run out of breath just over 140 mph, while I never met anyone, other than journalistic road-test teams who achieved an honest 150 mph with their E types. It was pretty academic anyway, even on German Autobahnen and Italian Autostrade, because traffic was beginning to clog up Europe by this time, though it would have been nice to get a maximum of 150 mph when the occasion presented itself. One or two racing people I knew made a habit of cruising at 125–130 mph between Milan and Modena, for example, but soon found they ran into tyre troubles and overheating after an hour or more. For the less sporting customer these problems did not arise.

I would have liked an E type coupé, from the

looks, performance and all-British aspect, but I could not see it standing up to the rough usage involved in trips to Sicily, Sweden or Portugal. I was aware that Jaguar knew all about the Le Mans 24 Hour race, or the 12 Hour race at Reims, but they had not convinced me that they could

In silhouette the E type coupé presented an outstanding shape and elegance of line that would be hard to improve upon. It is truly 'the car that is doing 100 mph when it is stationary'

cope with 1000 kilometres round the Nürburgring or round Monza, the 1000 miles of the Mille Miglia, or the 14 laps of the Targa Florio, all of which are guaranteed to destroy a GT car if it is not well designed and well-built. Firms like Porsche, Mercedes-Benz, Lancia or Ferrari gave

Above *The E type soon appeared on the racing circuits in the lighter roadster form. Here is Graham Hill driving the first E type to win a race (ECD400). Note that the central bar across the radiator opening has been removed to assist cooling*

Right *Roy Salvadori in action at Oulton Park in the famous white roadster 3.8 litre (BUY1) of Jaguar agent* John Coombs. By today's standards the car looks rather high off the ground and ungainly

the customer confidence; Jaguar did not. If you knew nothing of racing then it was a different story, you bought the car on its showroom merits and its price, and on those scores you did not hesitate to choose an E type, if that was your category of motoring. Mind you, a lot of people bought E types even though it was not their

An E type roadster 3.8 litre at speed at Silverstone in 1961

motoring style, and the Pop-fervour of the sixties bred just the sort of money and people that simply had to have an E type, even though they were never going to drive outside of London. It says a lot for the car that it was quite capable of being used around London day in and day out without protesting, for that lovely twin-cam 6-cylinder was so flexible and had huge reserves of torque so that it would pull top gear down to a walking pace.

I had forgotten all about the E type Jaguar from a personal viewpoint until one evening towards the end of 1964 when I was scuttling along in my Porsche, on local roads, when I became aware of some dipped headlights behind me that were staying with me round all the bends. On one particularly tricky left-hander which I knew well I really cornered on the limit, and still those headlights were behind me. That made me think a bit and I was intrigued to know what it was that was following me. On the next straight I eased off and an E type coupé went by . . .! That gave me cause to think and a short while later there was a chance to borrow a new Series 1 coupé, which had just been released for road-test. This had the new 4.2-litre engine and the new all-synchromesh Jaguar gearbox as well as numerous other improvements to seats, brakes, lights, electrics and so on. After a good run to the West of England and back I decided that a 4.2-litre E type was to be my next car. As it turned out I was to motor by E type for the next 15 years, using up a 4.2-litre Series 1 coupé and a 4.2-litre Series 2 roadster.

Left *The special Lightweight E type built for Briggs Cunningham for the 1964 Le Mans 24 Hour race. It was based on a standard roadster*

Overleaf Left *The impressive data sheet from the first* Autocar *road-test of an early 3.8 litre coupé showing the 150 mph timed maximum speed and 100 mph from rest in 16.2 seconds*

Overleaf Right *The* Motor *road-tested a roadster model in 1961 which matched the* Autocar *test figures remarkably closely*

JAGUAR E-TYPE GRAND TOURING COUPE

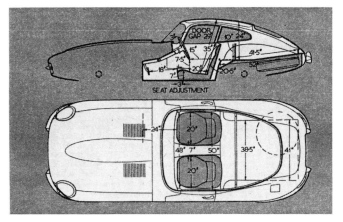

Scale ⅛in. to 1ft. Driving seat in central position. Cushions uncompressed.

DATA

PRICE (basic), with fixed head coupé body, £1,550.
British purchase tax, £646 19s 2d.
Total (in Great Britain), £2,196 19s 2d.
Extras: Chromium plated wire wheels, £60 4s 2d inc. P.T. Dunlop R.5 racing tyres: price to be announced later.

ENGINE: Capacity, 3,781 c.c. (230·6 cu. in.).
Number of cylinders, 6.
Bore and stroke, 87 × 106 mm (3·42 × 4·17in.).
Valve gear, twin overhead camshafts.
Compression ratio, 9 to 1.
B.h.p., 265 (gross) at 5,500 r.p.m. (b.h.p. per ton laden 195·4).
Torque, 260 lb. ft. at 4,000 r.p.m.
M.p.h. per 1,000 r.p.m. in top gear, 23·0 R.S.5; 24·6 R.5.

WEIGHT (with 5 gal fuel): 24·1 cwt (2,702lb).
Weight distribution (per cent): F, 49·6; R, 50·4.
Laden as tested, 27·1 cwt (3,038 lb).
Lb per c.c. (laden), 0·80.

BRAKES: Dunlop discs, inboard at rear. Hydraulic with vacuum servo, separate systems front and rear.
Disc diameter: F, 11in.; R, 10in.
Swept area: F, 242 sq. in.; R, 219 sq. in. (340 sq. in. per ton laden).

TYRES: 6·40 × 15in. Dunlop R.S.5.
Pressures (p.s.i.): F, 23; R, 25 (normal). F, 30; R, 35 (fast driving).
(Optional) Dunlop R.5: F (6·00 × 15in.), 35; R (6·00 × 15in.), 40 (maximum speeds).

TANK CAPACITY: 14 Imperial gallons (63·6 litres).
Oil sump, 11 pints (6·2 litres).
Cooling system, 22 pints (12·5 litres).

DIMENSIONS: Wheelbase, 8ft 0in. (243·8 cm).
Track: 4ft 2in. (127 cm).
Length (overall): 14ft 7·3in. (445·3 cm).
Width: 5ft 5·2in. (165·6cm).
Height: 4ft 0in. (122cm).
Ground clearance, 5·0in. (12·7cm).
Frontal area, 15 sq. ft. (approximately).

ELECTRICAL SYSTEM: 12-volt; 57 ampère-hour battery.
Headlamps, 60-60 watt bulbs.

SUSPENSION: Front, wishbones, torsion bars, telescopic dampers.
Rear, independent, transverse tubular and trailing links, twin coil springs and telescopic dampers each side, anti-roll bar.

PERFORMANCE

ACCELERATION TIMES (mean):
Speed range, Gear Ratios, and Time in Sec.

m.p.h.	3·31 to 1	4·25 to 1	6·16 to 1	11·18 to 1
10—30	—	—	3·2	1·9
20—40	5·5	4·3	2·8	1·9
30—50	5·4	4·3	2·8	—
40—60	5·5	4·3	3·0	—
50—70	5·4	4·1	3·1	—
60—80	5·6	4·1	—	—
70—90	5·8	4·5	—	—
80—100	6·1	4·9	—	—
90—110	6·3	6·0	—	—
100—120	7·2	—	—	—
110—130	8·5	—	—	—

From rest through gears to:

		m.p.h.	
30 m.p.h.	..	2·8 sec	
40 ,,	..	4·4 ,,	
50 ,,	..	5·6 ,,	
60 ,,	..	6·9 ,,	
70 ,,	..	8·5 ,,	
80 ,,	..	11·1 ,,	
90 ,,	..	13·2 ,,	
100 ,,	..	16·2 ,,	
110 ,,	..	19·2 ,,	
120 ,,	..	25·9 ,,	
130 ,,	..	33·1 ,,	

Standing quarter mile 14·7 sec.

MAXIMUM SPEEDS ON GEARS (R.5 tyres):

Gear			m.p.h.	k.p.h.
Top	(mean)		150·4	242·1
	(best)		151·7	244·2
3rd	..	..	116	187
2nd	..	..	78	125
1st	..	..	42	68

TRACTIVE EFFORT (by Tapley meter):

		Pull (lb per ton)	Equivalent gradient
Top	..	360	1 in 6·1
Third	..	520	1 in 4·2
Second	..	755	1 in 2·8

SPEEDOMETER: m.p.h.

	10	20	30	40	50	60	70	80	90	100	110	120	130	136
Car speedometer ..	10	20	30	40	50	60	70	80	90	100	110	120	130	136
True Speed. R. 5s ..	11	22	32	42	52	62	72	83	93	104	115	126	—	—
True Speed. R.S. 5s ..	10	20	30	41	51	61	72	82	92	102	113	124	135	140

BRAKES (at 30 m.p.h. in neutral)

Pedal load in lb	Retardation	Equiv. stopping distance in ft
25	0·20g	151
50	0·43g	70
75	0·64g	47
100	0·84g	36
115	0·87g	34·7

FUEL CONSUMPTION: (at steady speeds)

	Top Gear
30 m.p.h.	32·0 m.p.g.
40 ,,	32·5 ,,
50 ,,	30·5 ,,
60 ,,	28·2 ,,
70 ,,	26·5 ,,
80 ,,	24·5 ,,
90 ,,	22·5 ,,
100 ,,	19·0 ,,
110 ,,	16·5 ,,

Overall fuel consumption for 1,891 miles, 17·9 m.p.g. (15·8 litres per 100 km).
Approximate normal range 16-21 m.p.g. (17·6-13·5 litres per 100 km).
Fuel: Super Premium.

TEST CONDITIONS:
Weather: Dry, sunny, still air for maximum speed runs.
Air temperature, 41·7 deg. F.
Model described 17 March 1961.

STEERING: Turning circle:
Between kerbs: R, 40ft 5in.; L, 38ft 5in.
Between walls: R, 42ft 0in.; L, 40ft 0in.
Turns of steering wheel lock to lock, 2·75.

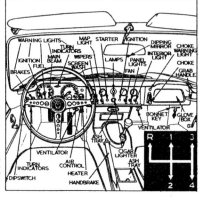

Make: Jaguar **Type:** E-type

Makers: Jaguar Cars, Ltd., Coventry, England.

Test Data

CONDITIONS: *Weather: Dry, warm, wind negligible. (Temperature 63°F. Barometer 30.5 in. Hg.). Surface: Dry tarmacadam. Fuel: Italian "Super" grade pump petrol (98-100 Octane Rating by Research Method).*

INSTRUMENTS

Speedometer at 30 m.p.h.	6% slow
Speedometer at 60 m.p.h.	1% fast
Speedometer at 90 m.p.h.	1% fast
Speedometer at 120 m.p.h.	accurate
Distance recorder	2½% slow

WEIGHT

Kerb weight, (unladen, but with oil, coolant and fuel for approx. 50 miles)	24 cwt.
Front/rear distribution of kerb weight	51/49
Weight laden as tested	28 cwt.

MAXIMUM SPEEDS

Flying Quarter Mile

Mean of opposite runs ..	..149.1 m.p.h.
Best one-way time equals ..	..150.1 m.p.h.

"Maximile" speed. (Timed quarter mile after one mile accelerating from rest.)

Mean of opposite runs ..	..136.4 m.p.h.
Best one-way time equals ..	..136.4 m.p.h.

Speed in gears (at 5,500 r.p.m.)

Max. speed in 3rd gear	107 m.p.h.
Max. speed in 2nd gear	74 m.p.h.
Max. speed in 1st gear	40 m.p.h.

FUEL CONSUMPTION

(Direct top gear)

25 m.p.g. at constant 30 m.p.h. on level.
27 m.p.g. at constant 40 m.p.h. on level.
27½ m.p.g. at constant 50 m.p.h. on level.
27½ m.p.g. at constant 60 m.p.h. on level.
26½ m.p.g. at constant 70 m.p.h. on level.
24 m.p.g. at constant 80 m.p.h. on level.
22½ m.p.g. at constant 90 m.p.h. on level.
21 m.p.g. at constant 100 m.p.h. on level.
17½ m.p.g. at constant 110 m.p.h. on level.
14½ m.p.g. at constant 120 m.p.h. on level.
13½ m.p.g. at constant 130 m.p.h. on level.

Overall Fuel Consumption for 2,859 miles, 144.9 gallons, equals 19.7 m.p.g. (14.35 litres/100 km.).

Touring Fuel Consumption (m.p.g. at steady speed midway between 30 m.p.h. and maximum, less 5% allowance for acceleration) 21.3.

Fuel tank capacity (maker's figure). 14 gallons

STEERING

Turning circle between kerbs:

Left	39 ft.
Right	36½ ft.
Turns of steering wheel from lock to lock	2½

BRAKES from 30 m.p.h.

1.00 g retardation (equivalent to 30 ft. stopping distance) with 115 lb. pedal pressure.
0.96 g retardation (equivalent to 31 ft. stopping distance) with 100 lb. pedal pressure.
0.79 g retardation (equivalent to 38 ft. stopping distance) with 75 lb. pedal pressure.
0.49 g retardation (equivalent to 61 ft. stopping distance) with 50 lb. pedal pressure.
0.22 g retardation (equivalent to 136 ft. stopping distance) with 25 lb. pedal pressure.

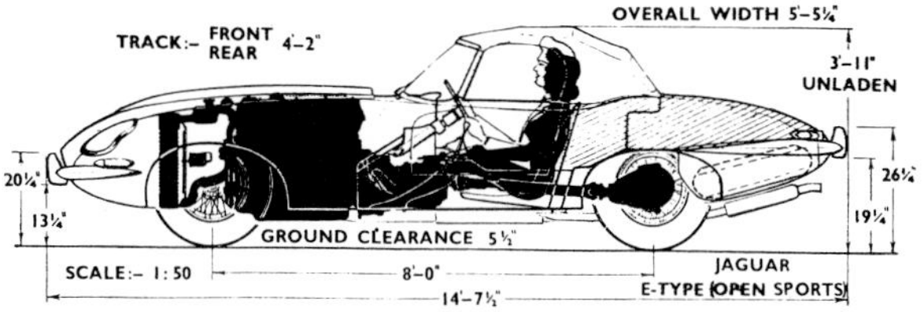
OVERALL WIDTH 5'-5¼"
TRACK:- FRONT REAR 4'-2"
3'-11" UNLADEN
20¼"
13¼"
26¼"
19¼"
GROUND CLEARANCE 5½"
SCALE:- 1:50
8'-0"
14'-7½"
JAGUAR E-TYPE (OPEN SPORTS)

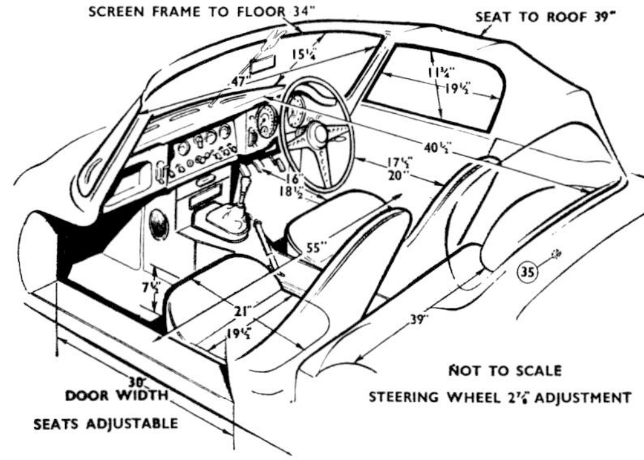
SCREEN FRAME TO FLOOR 34"
SEAT TO ROOF 39"
15¼"
47"
11¼"
19½"
40½"
17½"
20"
16"
18½"
55"
35
7½"
21"
19½"
39"
30"
DOOR WIDTH
SEATS ADJUSTABLE
NOT TO SCALE
STEERING WHEEL 2⅞" ADJUSTMENT

ACCELERATION TIMES from standstill

0-30 m.p.h.	2.6 sec.
0-40 m.p.h.	3.8 sec.
0-50 m.p.h.	5.6 sec.
0-60 m.p.h.	7.1 sec.
0-70 m.p.h.	8.7 sec.
0-80 m.p.h.	11.1 sec.
0-90 m.p.h.	13.4 sec.
0-100 m.p.h.	15.9 sec.
0-110 m.p.h.	19.9 sec.
0-120 m.p.h.	24.2 sec.
0-130 m.p.h.	30.5 sec.
0-140 m.p.h.	39.3 sec.
Standing quarter mile	15.0 sec.

ACCELERATION TIMES on Upper Ratios

	Top gear	3rd gear
10-30 m.p.h.	5.6 sec.	4.2 sec.
20-40 m.p.h.	5.6 sec.	4.3 sec.
30-50 m.p.h.	5.4 sec.	4.0 sec.
40-60 m.p.h.	5.4 sec.	4.0 sec.
50-70 m.p.h.	5.3 sec.	3.9 sec.
60-80 m.p.h	5.0 sec.	3.7 sec.
70-90 m.p.h.	5.2 sec.	4.2 sec.
80-100 m.p.h.	5.7 sec.	4.8 sec.
90-110 m.p.h.	6.6 sec.	6.5 sec.
100-120 m.p.h.	7.7 sec.	—
110-130 m.p.h.	10.4 sec.	—
120-140 m.p.h.	15.1 sec.	—

HILL CLIMBING at sustained steady speeds

Max. gradient on top gear	1 in 5 (Tapley 440 lb./ton)
Max. gradient on 3rd gear ..	1 in 3.7 (Tapley 585 lb./ton)
Max. gradient on 2nd gear ..	1 in 2.4 (Tapley 860 lb./ton)

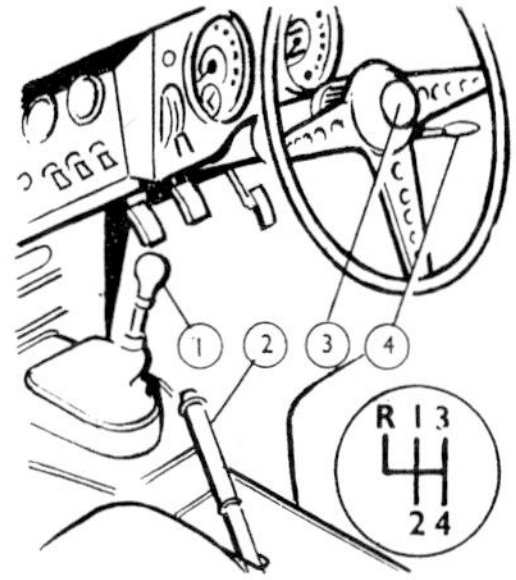
1
2
3
4
R 1 3
2 4

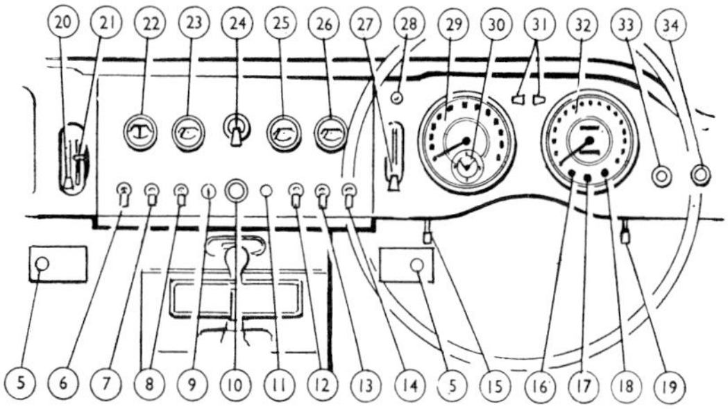
20 21 22 23 24 25 26 27 28 29 30 31 32 33 34
5 6 7 8 9 10 11 12 13 14 5 15 16 17 18 19

1, Gear lever. 2, Handbrake. 3, Horn button. 4, Direction indicator and headlamp flasher control. 5, Vent flaps. 6, Interior lights switch. 7, Bright-Dim panel light switch. 8, 2-speed heater fan control. 9, Ignition switch. 10, Cigar lighter. 11, Starter 12, Map light switch. 13, 2-speed windscreen wipers control. 14, Electric screen washer control. 15, Clock adjuster. 16, Ignition warning light. 17, Fuel warning light. 18, Headlamp warning light. 19, Trip reset. 20, Fresh air control. 21, Heater control. 22, Ammeter. 23, Fuel gauge. 24, Lights switch. 25, Oil pressure gauge. 26, Water thermometer. 27, Choke. 28, Choke warning light. 29, Rev counter. 30, Clock. 31. Direction indicator warning lights. 32, Speedometer. 33, Handbrake and hydraulic fluid level warning light. 34, Dip switch. 35, Boot lid control (see middle drawing).

Chapter 2
3.8 litre good...

What was it that changed my feelings about the E type? I was looking for a new car to replace my Porsche and after ten years of air-cooling and rear-engines I thought that if I was going to change I should do something drastic and start a whole new life of motoring. To go to a front engine and water cooling was the first big step, and to go from a small compact little sporting coupé to a large, almost cumbersome touring coupé was the next step. But there was more to it than that. The E type had appealed to me from the beginning but did not match up to my requirements on a number of small, but important details. I found in the revised 4.2-litre that most of those had been eradicated. The engine had been enlarged to 4.2-litre by increasing the bore from 87 mm to 92.07 mm, not by a simple boring-out process but by a complete re-design of the cylinder block with different spacing between the bore centre-lines. This enlarged engine gave a better torque figure and even greater smoothness though the actual output in bhp was unchanged. People who were using the E type for competition work preferred the old 3.8-litre power unit as it was more responsive to fine tuning and would rev higher, but for general use the 4.2-litre was a nicer engine. To this new version of the twin-cam six-cylinder Jaguar had mated an entirely new gearbox, with synchromesh on all four gears, a shorter lever travel and to me, now totally acceptable. Point number one eradicated. New seats had been designed, correcting all the faults of the 3.8-litre E type, and I subsequently found them perfect for a 12-hour driving stint. More seat movement had been provided, but this was not important to me as leg room is something I have never needed, having been at the back of the queue when legs were given out. The early bellows-type brake servo, which gave a quite a lot of trouble, was replaced by a much better vacuum-servo system, though the brakes were still by Dunlop. The electrical system had been changed totally and Joseph Lucas had allowed Jaguar to move into a new world of electrics. This came about by the change from DC dynamo to AC alternator, and

Engine view of an early 4.2 litre. This is a left-hand drive car as instanced by the brake and clutch fluid reservoirs mounted by the heater fan, with heat shield to protect them from the exhaust manifold. The alternator by the front exhaust manifold has no such luxury and suffered in consequence

Above *The revised instrument panel on the 4.2. This view shows the higher and broader backs to the vastly improved seats. The vertical struts in the foreground are restraints for luggage placed on the folded down rear floor*

Right *The cockpit of the 4.2. Note new seats and the short gear lever of the new all-synchromesh gearbox*

with it came all manner of improvements. The headlamps could now use 75 watt beams without flattening the battery, as the alternator could cope with the situation, which the old dynamo could not, and there was electrical power to spare. The headlamps combined to give you 150 watts to light your way, and did it very well. The rear window of the coupé now had a heater element in it, which was a godsend, for without heat on the rear window it misted up badly and you could not reach back from the driving seat to wipe it, the distance being too far. Lucas also provided a vastly improved starter

Above *A 4.2 litre coupé being hurried round a bend during road-testing by the* Motor *magazine. Note that the rear quarter-light is open to assist cooling of the cockpit, a system that the author found unacceptable due to wind-roar at 100 mph*

Right *The E type was the perfect foil for the advertising world of the 'swinging sixties', personifying speed and exhilaration. This is a National Benzole petrol company advertisement in the* Autocar *of 1966*

motor, with pre-engagement, that was so much sweeter to use than the old jangling vintage-type device used previously. Other electrical accessories like the petrol pump, the interior lighting, the instrument lighting and so on were improved as a consequence of the new alternator with its vastly superior output which started at a mere 920 rpm from the engine. Apart from small details the shape of the E type coupé remained unchanged, as well it might, for during its first four years of production it had not dated in the least and still represented speed and safety to the rest of the world. Or as Jaguar advertising said 'Grace . . . Space . . . Pace'.

Having established the 150 mph syndrome, which had become accepted by everyone, no great

play was made about speed with the 4.2-litre cars, they were merely said to be enlarged, improved and even better E types than the original models of 1961, which was true enough. The new E type was, in fact, no faster than the original car, the extra torque being used to overcome the inevitable increase in weight.

My order went in for a 4.2-litre coupé. Delivery was promised for the beginning of March, and sure enough it was delivered to my local garage on 11 March 1965. I was away testing a Marcos 1800 at the time—when I got back there was my sparkling new Carmen red 4.2-litre coupé (FPL660C). I had specified red as it is a colour that stands out against any background and I intended to use the car for high-speed motoring all over France, Italy, Spain and Germany and my many European motoring friends had instilled into me that it was most important to be seen when motoring fast, unlike today's situation when high speed has to be totally unobservable. Car colours that blend into the scenery were most undesirable for fast motoring. As my motoring was going to embrace countries like Spain, Yugoslavia, Sweden and even North Africa, I decided to have 8:1 compression pistons fitted, instead of the more normal 9:1, so that I would never have to bother about the enormous variations in the quality of petrol. With lots of long fast roads in view I selected the optional 3.07:1 rear axle ratio (3.31:1 was still standard at the time but actually only for another month) and specified the Salisbury Powr-Lok limited-slip differential, more for the comforting knowledge that I could then extract myself from muddy car parks at race meetings, than the need to eliminate wheelspin out of corners, for the E type independent rear suspension gave excellent traction under all conditions on dry roads. I also specified

left-hand drive and a metric speedometer as the car was going to spend most of its life in Europe.

There were 238 kilometres on the odometer when I took possession of the car and when I finally parted with it, at the end of 1969, the odometer had been right round once, and three-quarters towards the second time round! In all I covered 176,000 kilometres (109,300 miles) in that Carmen red coupé. It led a very hard life, but seemed to thrive on it, probably because it never really had a chance to cool down. It was in continual use under all sorts of conditions, seldom kept under cover, and travelling from ice and snow to Sicilian heat. The bodywork and paintwork proved exemplary throughout its life.

A 4.2 litre coupé with American style white-wall tyres. A wide-angle lens has distorted the lines of the car to exaggerate the length of the engine cover

The Browns Lane factory on the outskirts of Coventry with the entrance and reception area to the right, off Browns Lane itself. In the centre is the main assembly area

The initial running-in was no problem, as 60–70 mph was an easy unstrained pace. Local running and trips to Silverstone soon got the mileage up, and then the E type got a taste of what it was in for. I was due to drive in the Mobil Economy Run (for my sins) so I set off for the North of England on a journey that saw rain, rain and more rain, then sleet, slush and snow before I got to the start. Here the E type was left out in the snow while I did the event in a Singer Vogue (yes, really). While this initial running-in was being done I found it all too easy to put 100 miles into two hours, without going over 3000 rpm. The leisurely gait of the Jaguar on its high axle ratio was remarkably restful, so you really covered the ground without effort.

Other motoring activities delayed my first trip to Europe in the E type, so by the time I set off I had 2500 kilometres (1550 miles) on the clock and everything was nicely bedded in. As soon as I had got the car I had gone over it with a set of spanners, tweaking everything up just that little bit tighter than it had been done at the factory. I talked to one of the Jaguar engineers about this and he agreed that it was no bad thing, for on the assembly line things are done up to a 'production tightness' which tends to be nearer to the minimum than the maximum permissible. It seemed to pay off, for in more than 200,000 miles of E type motoring I never had anything fall off due to coming loose. The only bits that fell off were due to breakage or fatigue, but more of that later. That first trip was a fairly brief run to the Pyrenees and back, but the long straights after Bordeaux allowed me to get into the rhythm of effortless cruising at 100 mph, and I realized I was going to enjoy living with an E type.

The author concentrating on where he is going at 105 mph on an Italian Autostrada, photographed by his friend Peter Coltrin on the way to Sicily for the Targa Florio in 1966

The author displaying the handful of money (French Francs) needed to fill the E type fuel tank on a journey through France in 1966. A mere trifle compared to 1982

The next trip was a bit more serious, for it was straight down to Sicily, putting in an easy 500–600 miles a day. The ride and comfort of the E type was first class, the seats came up to all the claims made by Jaguar when they were introduced. On the Italian Austrade a leisurely gait was 105 mph, for at that speed you ease the accelerator pedal back and cruise on the minimum throttle opening, getting 20–22 mpg. If you wanted to cruise at 110 mph you had to have the throttle visibly open, not only did this raise the consumption to 18 mpg but it was tiring to the right foot. On all long-distance motoring I have found that cars settle in

The author's 4.2 litre coupé being refuelled in Spain. Note that the pump is at right-angles to 'normal' so that you can see it as you arrive thus making choice easier

to a pace that blends in with your own comfort, and the difference of 5 mph on the cruising speed of the E type made a remarkable difference in all respects. I found all day at 105 mph adequate for my needs.

From Sicily I spent the next three months motoring around Italy, France, Germany, Switzerland and Belgium and by the time I returned to base I had put another 12,000 kilometres (7500 miles) on the clock. The car had never missed a beat, I had greased it, changed its oil and done routine servicing, the only untoward job I had to do was to clean out the petrol-filter bowl,

45

which had gathered the muck from a wide variety of petrols. During that time I rotated the original Dunlop tyres around and later, as they wore thin, I changed over to Goodyear G800, which I found gave a much nicer feel to the car and certainly gave more confidence in the wet. By this time the front brake pads had worn out, so these were replaced. When I returned home the car had long passed the 10,000 mile mark and I was more than satisfied, for I put that figure as the minimum one should achieve without anything going wrong with a new car. It had been an instant starter at all times, even after being left at an airport in the open for a week. The fuel consumption had seldom dropped below 18 mpg, even when spending a day in second and third gears in mountain country, while a consumption on the right side of 20 mpg for long high-speed cruising was most impressive.

During this trip I had frequent occasion to use the full potential of the E type's 265 bhp (SAE), which in reality is an honest 180 bhp. I often pulled 5000 rpm in top gear (about 132 mph) reaching an absolute terminal of 143 mph on the long Autostrada straight past Montecassino, south of Naples. Not unnaturally one frequently became embroiled in private dices with Ferraris and other fast cars, and on one occasion I ran in company with a 250GT Ferrari at close on 120 mph from Milan to Turin, trying to overlook my extra 1.2 litres. Traffic was still scarce enough to render this possible in the mid-nineteen sixties, though it was beginning to increase visibly throughout Europe, and there were already areas you avoided assiduously. German Autobahn travel was a good way of covering the ground, providing all the other users behaved themselves, but on one trip south to Switzerland a Shell petrol tanker tangled with a VW Beetle, overturned and caught fire. We sat for two hours waiting for that mess to be cleared

up, for there was no way by and no way off the Autobahn. Once clear, and on to the deserted stretch from Baden-Baden to Basle I was able to make up some time and ran in company with a Porsche 90 at my usual cruising speed, with plenty in hand to get clear of impending trouble. At 105 mph the E type engine was turning over at 4000 rpm, which was right on the peak of the torque curve at a massive 283 ft lb, so that at that speed you had a lot of urge available if you floored the

The author's 4.2 litre Series One coupé having a service in a lay-by in Southern Italy. The Castrol oil is being changed and the suspension greased and routine checks made on battery, water, gearbox oil etc. Continuous use of the car precluded time for garages to carry out servicing

An enforced stop at a level-crossing in Sicily while returning from a Targa Florio, allowed time to chat to the two German enthusiasts in their 1935 Type 319 BMW

accelerator pedal, and for that sort of motoring acceleration at 100 mph was all important. You are naturally looking for a mile or more ahead and are 'reading the road' all the time, anticipating what might be going to happen so that if you can squirt up to 125 mph without effort you can get by an impending hazard before it develops, and then ease back to your cruising gait. It is all so much easier and more efficient than lifting off and standing on the brakes.

There were times when I contemplated changing the rear axle ratio for the optional 2.9:1, as against the 3.07:1 I was using, for the engine

would have certainly have had no difficulty pull-
ing it. I had occasion to try a friend's E type fitted
with the 2.9:1 ratio but it was a disappointment. It
was that little bit trickier to get away from rest,
but, more important, it put you too low down the
torque curve at 90–100 mph, and you lost that
wonderful surge forward with the nose rising up,
that you got with the 3.07:1 axle. You needed to
change down into third gear to get the best
performance, and that removed one of the charms
of the E type for long-distance motoring, I therefore decided that the 2.9:1 ratio was not for me.

As I have already mentioned, in those days (the
mid-sixties) there were no restrictions on speed
anywhere; it was not even frowned upon by 'do-
gooders' and I found that the front view of an E
type carried with it that 150 mph syndrome. Other
drivers would move over as soon as they saw you
in their rear-view mirror, for the frontal view could
not be confused with anything else, and the whole
world knew that the E type meant 150 mph. Even
if you were quietly cruising along at 70–80 mph
people would move over when you did not intend
to overtake. At times it was quite embarrassing,
for I did not always want to rush past, and you
could see the motorist in front wondering why the
E type did not go by. A pretty regular trip was
down the Autostrada from Milan to Modena, the
home of Maserati and Ferrari among lots of other
things. One of the best runs the E type did on this
stretch was 1 hour 3 minutes holding 5100 rpm in
top for a long way (about 135 mph). I doubt that it
would be possible today, under normal conditions, because of the traffic density, but seventeen
years ago the Italians were still chary of spending
money on using the Autostrada, and heavy lorries
were still using the old via Emilia and saving the
Toll money. Things are very different today and
the whole world is conscious that 'time-means-

When the snow lay on the ground, deep and crisp and even, the author took the opportunity of spinning his E type to get the feel of steering corrections at the limit and the dumbell effect of the relatively long car with weight masses at each end. This scene was on a deserted road in France. The wheel-tracks in the foreground were not made by the E type!

money' so the expensive-to-travel-on Autostrade are full of big trucks.

Many of the trips during those three months were done in torrential rain. 1965 was a record year for rain in Europe, and on one journey from Modena, over the Brenner Pass and through Germany to the Nürburgring I began to get a bit apprehensive about the legend of Noah and his Ark. The river Neckar was full to the brim and in places the Rhine had overflowed its banks so I splashed through numerous villages that were six inches or more deep in water. Through it all the E type never faltered though there was quite a bit of steam being generated as the exhaust pipes and silencers became submerged, but the upswept tail pipes stayed clear of the water. No water came in through the rear hinged panel, as many people told me it would. The triple windscreen wipers, that were peculiar to E types, worked overtime and the only problem I found was that the brakes filled up with water so that there was a heart-stopping delay when you applied the brakes, before the water was wiped off the disc. I was never brave (or stupid) enough to run in close company with heavy traffic on motor-ways in pouring rain, preferring to branch off over small roads on my own if the weather deteriorated beyond a certain level, so that this water on the brakes problem never gave me any trouble. During the following winter, however, I found the front brakes suffering from water and corrosion, because the car was never kept in a heated motor-house and was used in all weathers. In the depths of the winter the left front brake seized up solid, due to rust and corrosion, and was a rather tiresome job to free-up, rectify and fit new pads to the front brakes at the same time.

Chapter 3
...4.2 better

With its first European season finished, and 20,000 miles covered I gave the car a big service and the only adjustment I had to make was to take up a bit of slack on the camshaft timing chain, a simple matter providing you used the right tool for the job. As a matter of routine I changed the ignition points and the sparking plugs, just as I had done at 10,000 miles, for I feel that those items are so easily replaced that they are not worth messing about with.

On looking back it would seem that 25,000 miles would have been a good time to have traded the E type in for a new one, for as that figure approached all manner of small things went wrong. Nothing actually stopped me motoring, but there were annoying little things which affected total reliability. The drive-dog on the back of the inlet camshaft for the rev-counter unit broke, the alternator belt broke, one of the bonnet catches broke and the voltage control unit gave up, all within 4000 miles. The last was the most serious trouble that occurred, for the first noticeable symptom was a flat battery. I was in the South of France at the time and I assumed the battery had died of overwork, so I bought a new one and continued on my way to Italy but I noticed however, that the battery-charge indicator was showing rather a lot of 'charge'. Normally, when

The 4.2 litre E type coupé in typical touring country, high in the Swiss Alps. The grandeur of the background enhances the striking looks of the Jaguar

you started from cold the needle would go well over into 'charge' and after a few seconds would drop progressively back until it settled just to the plus side of the neutral mark. The Smiths instrument had no markings or graduations on it, so there was no telling how many amps the alternator was giving out at any time. I later found out that it was something like 45 amps when the needle was well into the plus side! Not surprisingly my new battery was soon boiling merrily, which I only noticed when I opened the bonnet to fiddle with the alternator. It was so hot that the pitch was almost fluid and had changed shape. As I was heading for Modena, where I knew all sorts of helpful people, I disconnected the alternator, by removing the driving belt and ran the rest of the way on the contents of my overfull battery, which did not seem to have suffered too much. An Italian electrical wizard diagnosed the trouble instantly. It was the little black box on the bulkhead, which was supposed to regulate the alternator output, so this meant a trip to Milan to get another one, which immediately put everything right.

After overcoming these small troubles everything settled down and total reliability became

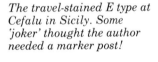

The travel-stained E type at Cefalu in Sicily. Some 'joker' thought the author needed a marker post!

British and proud of it. At an Italian refuelling stop the 4.2 litre E type coupé shows its smooth lines alongside the contemporary Ferrari 275GTB

the order of the day, with just routine oil changes, greasing and routine checking of things. I was in the throes of another three-month European trip, covering the ground from Cherbourg in the top left hand corner of France down to Syracuse in the bottom right hand corner of Sicily and all I seemed to do was to use up tyres and consume petrol and oil. Apart from the charging trouble nothing was touched, the engine just went on and on, and I never gave a thought to the gearbox or the rear axle. Tyre consumption varied from 6000 miles to 12,000 miles for a set of Goodyear G800s, depending on the sort of motoring. The long fast trips to Sicily where I cruised all day at 105 mph promoted increased wear, as opposed to leisurely motoring around Belgium and Germany, or in Switzerland. Traffic density in some parts was becoming intolerable though, especially in Switzerland, so it was quicker to make a 500 mile detour through France or Austria and enjoy the motoring than to get bogged down trying to cross that country in the height of the summer.

As 60,000 kilometres came up the exhaust system began to suffer and the first thing to happen was for the tail pipes to rust through and come adrift. The E type exhaust system was one of its worst points, for the two three-branch manifolds each fed into a down-pipe that went into its own silencer, these silencers being bolted up under the centre of the monocoque. In the down-pipes were flexible joints to allow the engine to waggle about on its rubber mountings, and the flexible bits rusted up and eventually split. The silencers themselves gave no trouble, but, aft of these, two long tail pipes ran under the rear suspension and then sloped upwards to two small silencers with short tail pipes. The first one of these tail pipes came off at 100 mph and skated up an Autobahn, and the other one was rusted through and ready to part company, so I threw it away and made up two straight-through pipes from the main silencers. There was no noticeable change in the exhaust note.

Front brake pads were wearing out pretty quickly, which was not surprising since they had plenty of work to do, slowing 2892 lbs (1317 kgs) continually from well over 100 mph, though I was not by any means a heavy braker. As with tyres you could tie in brake pad wear to the type of motoring, and the front ones needed changing between 9000 miles and 15,000 miles, and it was a pretty simple job to change them, a job I usually did in a hotel car park while on my travels. The rear pads were something else, with the brakes being mounted inboard, this task involved a lot of lying on the back with a lead light, and much cursing and swearing about the limited space available.

Above *Britain versus Italy. The 4.2 litre E type coupé alongside a contemporary Ferrari. The larger cross-sectional area of the Ferrari relative to the Jaguar is interesting, while the much wider wheel track of the Italian car is impressive*

Left *An English visitor to the Nürburgring had a 'moment' on the way which made an expensive mess of the side of his 3.8 litre coupé. It was a red car and for an awful moment the author thought someone had clobbered his car which was parked in the paddock*

Two and Two Plus Two. The new longer wheelbase 2+2 E type in front of a 2-seater coupé E type outside the South Kensington (London) Jaguar agents H. R. Owen Ltd. Note the longer door and side window on the 2+2 and its more upright windscreen

In the spring of 1966 a new model of the E type was introduced, aimed at the family man who wanted E type motoring but who was hampered with children. This was the 2+2 which was a lengthened version, nine inches being added to the wheelbase to bring it up to 8 ft 9 in., and providing space in the back for two small seats which could accommodate small children (or a dog!). In the normal coupé the space behind the seats was used for luggage, with the spare wheel under the floor in a recess beside the 14-gallon fuel tank. There was ample space for luggage in the two-seater but the only disadvantage was that it was exposed to full view through the rear window, and in some European countries the sight of a suitcase on the back floor was too much of a temptation for light-fingered gentry. On occasions when I left my E type at an airport or in a car

The interior of the 2+2 showing adequate seating space for children in the rear compartment. The upper half of the seat back folds forwards to provide a larger luggage area

park for any length of time, I used to put my suitcase and other small items in the spare-wheel well under the floor, and leave the spare wheel on the luggage platform, in full view, feeling that thieves were unlikely to be as attracted by a spare wheel like they would be by cases. Of course, they could have stolen the whole car, but that was another matter altogether.

To my mind the 2+2 model was not a great success, for its looks were spoilt by the elongated body, and to increase head-room the rake of the windscreen was made more upright so that in side elevation it lost all the sleekness of the normal two-seater coupé. As the width remained the same, the width to length aspect ratio was all wrong, for the normal E type was just about on the limit of aesthetic acceptability. Not being a family man, I never found out whether the 2+2

A car to be proud of. Sir William Lyons poses with a 4.2 litre Series 2 coupé. Note that the headlamps no longer have perspex covers and the hub-caps have lost their 'ears'

was what the family man wanted, though people did tell me it wasn't. I did a fairly long test-trip in a 2+2, not because I thought I might want one, but to keep in touch with what Jaguar were doing. Personally I did not like the feel of the longer wheelbase, and there was an unpleasant tendency for the front to run-out on corners.

Before the end of my second year with the 4.2 the alternator gave up the ghost and needed replacing, I then discovered that you had to pay heavily for the surplus of electricity over the old-fashioned dynamo. A new alternator cost more than twice as much as a dynamo, and it had failed because the silicon-diodes had overheated and burnt out. There was no way of repairing it. Reading some text books on alternators I discovered that the last thing the diodes enjoyed was

The change over from Series One to Series Two cars saw some models termed Series 1½ in which a few detail changes were not finished. In this cockpit view of a Series 1½ the clock is still in the tachometer and a push-button starter switch is still in use

external heat and Jaguar mounted their alternator just above the forward exhaust manifold!
This was not from choice but from expediency, for
it was very crowded under the bonnet of the E
type and the layout was designed long before the
alternator came into being. After some years they
did get round to putting a small heat-shield round
the alternator, but it was only a token gesture.

Before starting my third European season with
the car 50,000 miles came up so I decided to let the
factory service department have a look at it, just
in case anything needed doing before yet another
summer of hard work. The major part of the
engine was not touched, but the cylinder head
was changed for one with better oil control for the
valve guides, which drastically reduced oil consumption, a major problem with the 4.2-litre
engine from its inception. A new clutch was fitted
as a precautionary measure, as I felt that the
original one had done a lot of work. The gearbox

The 4.2 litre rear boot showing spare wheel, jack and tools stowed under the plywood left-out floor board. The petrol tank is under the fixed plywood floorboard on the left. A surprising amount of luggage (of the right shape) could be stowed well forward under the rear deck

was not touched as it was perfect, but the crownwheel and pinion were renewed, not because of undue wear but because Jaguar felt it had become noisy, though personally I was not aware of this. With the whole differential assembly hung on the bodywork there was inevitably more noise transmitted to the inside of the car, even though the axle sub-frame was mounted on rubber blocks, than with a non-independent rear axle where the diff assembly was hung on the springs. For about 5000 miles the car was uncannily quiet, just as it was when it was new, but then a faint whine could be heard coming from the rear axle. Sharp eared passengers reckoned they could hear it at 2000 miles, but I was sufficiently deaf to disagree with

Virtually no colour is unsuitable for the sleek E type. This one, a 1961 3.8 roadster, has chassis number '45'. Note Dunlop RS5 tyres and non-standard exhaust tailpipes. Beautiful even with the hood up

Right *A 3.8 coupé of 1964 vintage ('B' suffix registration sees to that) shows off its 'white-line' as opposed to white-wall tyres in the early evening. Perched high to today's eyes but still most striking. No wonder it created such a show back in 1961*

Right *This is a Series One 4.2 litre roadster. The original style exhaust tailpipes are clearly visible. Tyres are Dunlop SP41 radials*

Left *Still lovely, although now in Series Two trim with unfaired headlamps, under-bumper front side lamps and similar but larger rear. Knock-offs no longer have ears. 1965 4.2 litre version*

Above *Moody shot from the
Jaguar Cars agency in North
America. Now not so sleek
(Grace) nor so fast (Pace) but
perhaps more Space*

Right *The Two plus Two in
American specification. Still
4.2 litres but with side-
marker lights, driver's door
mirror and those 'white'
tyres. The shape, somehow,
doesn't seem too cluttered
although it's only 1969*

Far Right *The first of the
V12s being photographed in
November 1972 for American
publicity and promotional
purposes. Snow suggests
Coventry but in fact its
America's equally cold East
Coast*

Above *Contrasting factory hardtop for the Series Three V12 roadster makes the cockpit very snug*

Below *Often called the 'only production V12 in the world' Jaguar have every right to be proud of its success*

Right *Getting fatter all the time the V12 E type roadster still can be called lithe and sleek. More so than the Two plus Two. This mid-series car is in superb condition*

Right *The Series Three cockpit. There's still the traditional wood-rimmed steering wheel but the facia has taken to matt black and rocker switches*

Below *Racing in the 1980s dictates changes for the E type. That sleekness has gone only to be replaced by bulges, louvres and tubing. Champion Fred Baker is driving here in 1978*

It's 1967 and press test day for the Series 1½ 4.2 litre here at Zandvoort. It must have been the fastest car on the track

them! As I was about to set off on one of my long European trips I contacted a friend at Jaguar to see what he thought and his honest opinion was 'don't worry'. Another friend who had been running E Types since the 3.8-litre days said the same thing. His opinion was that the E type rear axle was built like the Forth Bridge and you would be hard-put to destroy it, a little noise did no-one any harm. I took their advice and carried on motoring and the noise got no worse, in fact it was still making it 100,000 kilometres later!

Until I started using a Jaguar I never really knew any Jaguar owners, or even noticed them, but once in the 'clan' I discovered a remarkable number of racing people were using E types and I was frequently meeting other owners in my travels. Some of them loved their cars and forgave them any idiosyncracies, while others were so upset that I wondered why they had ever bought their E type in the first place. One chap I crossed the Channel with on the Dover–Calais ferry had

73

only done 3000 miles in his and all manner of things seemed to have gone wrong, many I suspect due to his own unsympathetic handling of the car. He nit-picked about every little thing, many of them defects I had never even noticed with mine. After he had gone on his grumbling way I looked around my well-worn car and saw I had the troubles he had been complaining about, such as pitting on some of the chrome, slight imperfections in the paint around the wheel-arches, a stiff to operate choke control, typical rack-and-pinion kick-back in the steering, and so on. As I went on my 100 mph way I decided he spent more time looking at his car than driving it the way it was meant to go.

By the end of the third season my car was still going as well as ever, with never an involuntary stop. It was proving as amenable to long-distance fast motoring as it was to very slow pottering, for I often took time off from race-reportage to tour around remote parts of France and Italy, or over some of the more rugged Alpine passes, especially in the French Alps. On one mountainous trip across the centre of Sicily the clouds were right down on the ground and visibility was nearly zero. For three-quarters of an hour the E type was in second gear, running between 1000 and 1500 rpm and it just ticked quietly along in the most leisurely and comforting manner. A couple of days later it was spending all day at well over the 100 mph mark on its way north up the Auto-strada. On my favourite fast-stretch before Naples it reached 5800 rpm in top gear, running on some special low-profile tyres which lowered the over-all gear ratio a bit. Normally I found 5000 rpm quite fast and comfortable enough, for over that you began to become very conscious of those great 92.07 mm diameter pistons pounding up and down that long 106 mm stroke. For all normal purposes 4000–4500 rpm was quite adequate in the gears, for that took you right to the peak of the torque curve and to nearly 100 mph in third. A quick change into top gear and you were well on your way. At 5000 rpm or more there was a bit of a pandemonium going on under that long bonnet and I felt that continuous use of such revs in 2nd or 3rd gears was going to shake things to bits.

While on a visit to the Lotus factory in Norfolk during the summer of 1967 one of the Jaguar engineers was there in a Mark 10 saloon, a rather big and gormless luxury wagon in my estimation. He insisted that I let a colleague drive my E type and that I went with him on the journey from Norwich out to the Lotus factory. He would not say why, but as we set off I realized that this was no ordinary Mark 10. It got up and went like no Jaguar I had been in before, leaving my E type so far behind it was ridiculous. He refused to open the bonnet or talk about the car, but when no-one was about I lay underneath and saw the first Jaguar V12 engine!

Chapter 4
Coupé then roadster

These were the very early beginnings of the V12 Jaguar and it was all very secret and experimental, so that thoughts of a V12 road car never entered my head. I was really hoping that one day we would see a V12 racing-sports car to carry on the traditions of the D type. As we now know, we nearly did see that happen.

With the mileage on my car now well past the 70,000 mile mark I returned it to the factory for a check over before starting out on its fourth European season. They rectified various things that could have led to trouble. There were signs that water had been leaking past the cylinder head gasket, where it showed signs of corrosion, they looked at the bottom end and found slight score marks on the main bearing shells due to water intrusion. Pistons, rings and bores were all in good shape, so new main bearings shells and big end shells were fitted and a top-end overhaul was all that was needed. As a precaution a new set of exhaust valves were put in and the engine assembled with a new type of head gasket, to obviate the corrosion troubles, which the factory had been working on. Later on the cylinder head to block joint was revised, to solve this problem once and for all. The whole brake system was over-hauled, as was the front suspension, which needed new bushes and ball-swivels. New exhaust mani-folds were fitted, a new radiator as the old one was showing signs of cracking up, and the engine was fitted with the new type of square-section cambox covers, in place of the old rounded and polished ones which dated back to the XK120. It was interesting that these new cambox covers with their polished longitudinal fluting bore a close resemblance to covers used on the last of the Coventry-Climax racing engines. The Jaguar engineers Walter Hassan and Harry Mundy had both been at Coventry-Climax before it was amal-gamated with Jaguar. Naturally, during this overhaul consumable items such as water hoses, drive belts, filters and so on were all renewed, so that when the car set off abroad again it was like new. Each time it went to the Jaguar factory it came back with Champion sparking plugs fitted

The author used his E types in all weathers and on all terrain. Here the red coupé is at the top of the snow covered Col d'Allos in France

and each time I took them out and replaced them with Autolite AG42s. With the Champions I found that if you did a lot of town driving or slow running in mountain country, and then got out on the open road and began to pile on the steam there would be some hiccoughing over 4000 rpm until the plugs cleared, and then you would be away. They never missed a beat while pottering about, but I found it tiresome to have to 'clear' them before settling down to 100 mph cruising. The Autolite plugs never did this and you could come straight out of a big city like Paris or Milan, onto the open road and the engine would run straight up to 5000 rpm without any hesitation. The Champion people would never accept that their plugs were at fault and I was too busy to take them for a demonstration, anyway it was easier to fit Autolites and forget. Jaguar had a contract with Champion to supply plugs for original equipment as they did with Dunlop for tyres, but I did hear from round the back door at the factory that a lot of experimental work on the test-beds was done on Autolites!

The summer months of 1968 saw another 15,000 European miles added. The Jaguar just went on and on, consuming petrol, oil, brake pads and tyres but with never an involuntary stop. Throughout all the running I kept a detailed log-book of its activity, and 1968 was impressively drama free. As with the car when it was new, the new exhaust manifolds burnt off all their lovely black enamel finish on the first day of 100–110 mph continuous motoring and thereafter retained the normal brown rusty appearance of a hard-used engine. I always found it remarkable to look at some E type Jaguars with quite big mileages on the clock, yet still had the original black enamel on their exhaust manifolds, sure proof that the car had never been used as was

Above *A rather dramatic shot of the author's 4.2 litre coupé in Italian mountain country with low clouds obscuring the mountain peak*

Left *The frontal treatment of the Series Two E type, with raised and exposed headlamps, larger air intake opening for the radiator and larger sidelamp and winker clusters mounted under the bumpers. The stick-on number plate on E types was strictly illegal, being neither vertical nor on a flat surface, but reference to Sir William Lyons usually placated the law*

The Series Two instrument layout and fascia panel. A key-starter switch is now incorporated with a steering column lock to the left of the steering wheel centre, the clock has left the tachometer and is a much larger instrument in the centre of the panel and toggle switches have given way to tumbler switches. When pressed down for 'on' a white portion is revealed at the top providing quick visual confirmation of what is 'on'

intended. Similarly, if you looked under some E types you could see they had never been out of town or driven hard on all types of going. The telltale symptoms of hard usage were scratches and graunches along the underside of the twin central silencers, while the tail pipes under the rear suspension would be flattened. The suspension of the E type was so good that you could ride any undulations without the least worry as regards handling and stability, but you did have to pay for it with damage to the exhaust system, the lowest point on the car. It all stood it remarkably well,

An early Series Two car with exposed headlamps and small sidelamp/winker clusters. By 1982 standards for fast cars the tyres look incredibly 'skinny'

for on French B-roads it was happening continually. It was also a contributory factor to the frequency at which exhaust systems broke up, and I often contemplated making up a short system with side outlets, but never got round to it. Of course, I could have driven more slowly, but that seemed pointless with a car that handled and rode the undulations so superbly.

Apart from the usual fitting of new ignition points every 10,000 miles, I never looked at the engine and things like tappet adjustment were purely academic. Once set up properly, the

81

A Series Two roadster with the raised headlamps, later sidelamp clusters and mandatory 'navigational' lights and reflectors on the corners of the bodywork. Compared to 1961 cars the E type is beginning to get a 'cluttered up' look about it, all to comply with USA laws. The close-fitting hood which remained remarkably rigid even at 130 mph is clearly shown

Jaguar valve gear could be forgotten, though occasionally I used to take off the oil filler cap on the lefthand cambox with the engine on tick-over, just to look with pleasure at the vast flow of oil passing among the cams and valve buckets; it was most reassuring.

Parts of that summer of 1968 proved to be very hot in Europe, and I found the ventilation and cooling of the E type cockpit a bit lacking. The flow of cold air that came in through the ventilation system was not really adequate, but the worst thing was the generating of heat inside the car. After a few hours' running, the handbrake, mounted between the seats was like a single-bar electric fire in the heat that it transmitted up from the silencers and in addition the clever heated rear window, which was on automatically with the ignition, acted like another electric fire. The only cure was to open the rear quarter lights, or the main windows, but then the wind noise was unbearable at high speed. It never occurred to me to go more slowly! When everything was closed up the wind noise in the E type coupé was remarkably low, and the silence at 100 mph was not only impressive but also conducive to long-distance driving, for noise is very tiring. For this reasons I was not interested in having one of the proprietary sunshine siding roof panels fitted. As I was not prepared to drive slowly, or suffer unnecessary noise, I just wafted on my way perspiring profusely.

Putting 80 miles into the hour on the German Autobahnen was the normal order of things, and on one trip down to Switzerland I averaged 85 mph for two hours. It was still happy to show an honest 140 mph in bursts of enthusiasm, and 130 mph was always on hand to get rid of cars that insisted on sitting with you at 100–105 mph, the all-day and every day cruising speed. It was beginning to become increasingly difficult to shake off Citroën DS21 and BMW 2002 saloons. I often mused to myself about the ease with which I was travelling around Europe at the 100 mph mark, saying to myself 'this is ridiculous, you really should stop spending all day at 100 mph'. Little did I realize that the net of restrictions was soon to descend, the whole world was going to consider speeds of three figures as something immoral and illegal, high-speed motoring was soon to be outlawed and controlled by police and radar. We were in the happy 'swinging sixties' and all was well with the world.

*Towards the end. A 2+2
E type at the London Motor
Show fitted with bolt-on
pressed steel wheels. Wire
wheels had now become an
optional extra*

Above *This front view of a Series Two roadster shows clearly why the maximum speed was down. The exposed headlamps provided built-in head-winds, the much larger radiator intake aperture presented more drag*

Right *Rear end treatment of a Series Two roadster showing the massive rear light cluster. The exhaust tail pipes have been set more widely apart to allow a number plate to fit between them. The small light to the right of the over-rider is one of the reversing lights*

Long distances in the day were as easy as high speeds, and naturally the two went together, with no fear of retribution or the need to concentrate on anything other than driving nicely. Covering 1000 kilometres (620 miles) between breakfast and supper was no great strain and one of the fascinations about such travel was to have breakfast, lunch, tea and dinner in four different countries.

During the summer I was able to have a foretaste of what Jaguar were up to in their experimental department, and where Jaguar motoring was going. I was allowed a day out in a new saloon heavily disguised with taped-on cardboard sheets, which was a prototype XJ6. Although it seemed a big car compared with an E type, it presented a whole new world as regards comfort, ride, handling and stability, especially when compared to the old Mark 10. Although I did not appreciate it at the time, that experimental XJ6 was the forerunner of a whole new generation of Jaguar cars which were eventually to make the E type obsolete.

The Carmen red coupé lasted me one more season, by which time the total mileage was nudging 110,000 miles (176,500 kilometres), the majority of which were over roads of Europe under all conditions and speeds. I never once had to call for help and a tow-vehicle to reach my destination, which to me spells reliability. During the last year I got through another alternator (heat trouble again), had to unseize the brake calipers yet again, a perpetual battle with the Dunlop system, and one of the bonnet catches broke off and had to be welded at a roadside garage. While at base I renewed the universal joints in one of the drive shafts and replaced the bearings in the rear suspension on that side while I was at it.

Throughout its life it had never leaked a drop of

The Series Two E type 4.2 litre engine, showing the Coventry-Climax inspired cambox covers, the massive air filter and plenum chamber and the lack of a header tank behind the radiator. Expansion in the water system was accommodated by an overflow catch-tank mounted on the bulkhead on the left side

water into the cockpit, the rear hatch never sprung open as gloomy friends had predicted, and the gearbox was faultless. Personally I enjoyed the new Jaguar all-synchromesh baulk-ring gearbox, and though it did not have the slickness of a Porsche or a Ferrari gearbox, it was very pleasant to use and suited the characteristics of that big lazy 4.2-litre engine, with its maximum power at 5500 rpm. If you have an engine that revs to 7000 or 8000 rpm and sings happily to itself as it does it, then you need a really quick gear-change to be in sympathy with the engine. You have to be able to stir about from top to third and back in an instant, or snick into second, whirl the tachometer round into the red and then snick across into third, all without ever thinking. You did not drive an E

A 1970 Series Two E type coupé in standard form. The ultimate E type before detail changes took it 'over the top'

type like that, for torque was the keynote of the Jaguar engine and while the high-revver is stirring about in the gearbox, and enjoying it, you just opened the Jaguar throttle in whatever gear you happened to be in and 'whoosh', that 283 ft lb of torque wafted you away. Another fascinating aspect of the engine characteristics of the E type was its ability to pull away from rest with no throttle opening at all, with the rev-counter reading as low as 400 rpm. Without a sound you could ease away from rest without anyone knowing about it, which was quite useful at times, especially late at night! This same impressive low-speed torque was also enjoyable when turning round in a confined space, for you could ease backwards and forwards without touching the accelerator

A neatly arranged pair of Series Two E types showing the close affinity between the coupé and the roadster

pedal, the car moving either way on tick-over.

I never found the limit of adhesion during normal motoring, though now and again I got the whole thing sliding nicely on occasions in Sicily while 'playing bears' round the Targa Florio circuit, but it was a long car to get sideways on. When the opportunity arose, such as at an airfield, I did explore the limits of its cornering and found that once over the limit it was not at all happy and did little to help you regain control. It seemed as if it became embarrassed and said to itself 'I don't like this, I'm giving up', unlike some cars which stay with you to the bitter end. I took the opportunity on snow covered surfaces to spin the car deliberately, so as to find out how it reacted and how the steering behaved going from full-lock to full-lock, and for such a big car it was not all that bad.

It was during one of these sessions, in which I got it on full opposite-lock with the power hard on in second gear, so that it virtually pirouetted on its own centre of gravity, that a new noise appeared that I had not heard before. It was the dual electric cooling fans behind the radiator coming into operation. These cooling fans were controlled by a thermostat and in no time under normal conditions had the temperature risen high enough for the thermostat to switch the fans on. Pushing out quite a lot of power at zero mph had put the temperature up to the critical point. During my travels I met E type owners who were in awful trouble with their thermostatically controlled fans, either due to them not switching on and the radiator starting to boil, or due to them switching on too early and running virtually all the time. Perhaps I was lucky, but the electric motors of my fans were virtually unused when I sold the car.

No matter where the E type was photographed, or from what angle, it always presented an impressive picture. This is a 2+2 in a wild setting

Chapter 5
Times change

My motoring life was still going on so the questions was 'What next?'. After much thought I decided it would have to be another E type, and the Series 2 was now in production. It says a lot for the E type that after five years and over 100,000 miles I had not tired of it and was prepared to have another one. There was only one thing worrying me, and that was an uneasy feeling that began to grow during 1969 that the fun was over, that we were moving from the 'swinging sixties' into the 'sordid seventies' and that freedom of expression on the open road was going to disappear. The world was closing in on those of us who enjoyed fast 'E type' motoring, the age of the practical Eurobox for the peasant was fast approaching. The bicycle was fast disappearing. Traffic density was increasing by leaps and bounds, parts of Europe were becoming desperately clogged up, rules and regulations were appearing from all directions, and the scene was changing for the worse. Although I knew deep down that the 'seventies' were going to be very different, I tried to ignore the feeling and carry on as if it was still the nineteen fifties and sixties.

If you did not time things right you could spend an hour queueing up to cross a frontier, like that between Germany and Austria, or you could get bogged down behind rows of caravans on the slow winding roads in Switzerland and in parts of Italy you could be in amongst heavy commercial traffic for 50 miles or more before there was a hope of getting past. It was fast becoming necessary to search out small back routes to avoid traffic congestion, which though slow at least allowed you to keep moving, and some parts of Europe were only tolerable after midnight. Many of my friends had already succumbed to the changing conditions and given up serious motoring, but I decided it was not as bad as they made out and determined to carry on. As the scene was obviously going to be different I settled on an open two-seater roadster 4.2-litre E type as a replacement for the coupé, on the assumption that I could enjoy the sunshine if I got stuck in an Autobahn hold-up, or I could enjoy the scenery if I was on a slow winding detour. I chose a white one, to the same specification as before with 8:1 pistons and the 3.07:1 axle ratio, and the open-car aspect presented an entirely different motoring scene. I felt as if I was exploring an entirely new car,

The author about to start roadster-style E type motoring in his 4.2 litre of 1970

The author taking delivery of his Series Two roadster in pristine white with left-hand drive at the front entrance of the Browns Lane factory. It was not unusual to see Mr. Jaguar himself (Sir William Lyons) walking through the glass doors of the main entrance, for he was very much the head-man of the Jaguar empire and always about the place

rather than just another E type. It worked out well, for I found the roadster needed more looking after than the fixed head coupé, not in the way of maintainence or repair, but molly-coddling. When stopping for the night at an Hotel with the coupé I merely took my bag out, slammed the door, locked it and went into the hotel. Now I had to tuck the roadster up for the night, either put the tonneau cover on or the hood up, wind up the windows and make sure I left nothing in the cockpit that would attract thieves with a knife for slitting the tonneau or the hood. If a garage was

A Series Two roadster E type with hood erect, to American specification

available I would actually put the car away for the night, whereas with the coupé I just left it where it came to rest at the end of the day's motoring.

I had collected the roadster (BJD147H) direct from the Jaguar factory at the beginning of April in 1970 with 226 kilometres on the clock, and two days later I set off for a month's trip through France, Spain, Italy, Sicily and Belgium. Before leaving I had a tonneau cover made that could be unzipped down the centre, keeping the passenger seat covered and the driver's seat open. This I found essential when motoring with the hood down in that I could spread maps and papers on the passenger seat and they stayed there. Without the tonneau it was impossible. It also kept the cockpit much warmer, and I found that even in quite cold weather it was very comfortable with the heater going, obviating the need for scarves, rally jackets or gloves. Jaguar did not supply a tonneau cover for the roadster, as they were loath to spoil the nice bodywork with 'lift-dot' fasteners and fittings. When I suggested that it was 1970 and by now someone should have invented a better way of fastening a tonneau cover than the Edwardian method of metal fasteners, they simply replied that company policy did not embrace tonneau covers for open roadsters. I had my bodywork spoilt by drilling holes and screwing in metal fasteners, but I would not have had it any other way. If you stopped for a quick lunch or coffee, you did not want to mess about putting the hood up, even though it was pretty easy. It was so much easier to zip the tonneau across, and if you didn't you could be sure it would rain while you were away. Naturally I found snags with a tonneau cover, the worst one being that when left out in heavy rain two large pools of water would gather, one over each seat, and when they were full enough they would join in the middle and the water would pour in through the zip fastener. If you were parked at an angle forward, the water would run down over the instrument sill and fill the interior. I often returned after minor cloudbursts to find two inches of water swilling about in the footwells, but the searing sunshine of the South of France or Italy would soon dry everything out, even if you did have to leave the car looking like a second-hand carpet dealer with everything spread out over the bonnet to dry off. With the hood and sidewindows wound up, the

Above *Export Series Two coupé in the studio. Popular white 'rim' tyres of the period*

Left *Series Two 2+2 photographed by Andrew Whyte on a trip to Geneva. Better in a dark colour?*

Before the paint was scratched. The author's 4.2 litre roadster at a lunch stop on its maiden voyage to Spain during its running-in period

cockpit was reasonably water-tight, though if you did not make sure that the hood was seated properly on the top rail of the windscreen, water would cascade in. When putting the hood up in a hurry, as a cloudburst descended, this was easier said than done, and I spent many a mile mopping up water with a sponge, but it was all part of the joy of open-car motoring! The three over-centre catches that held the hood to the top of the windscreen were incredibly efficient and held everything tautly in place, even at 130 mph, but by golly you had to have strong fingers to pull them down into position and I doubt whether the average woman would ever have managed it. One tiresome little quirk of putting the hood up or down was that you had to tip both seats forward, otherwise the hood irons spiked the backs of the seats on their way by. This meant that it was impossible to raise or lower the hood from the driving seat, which was a pity. All part of open-air motoring, which I knew was going to be different. The view in the central rear-view mirror was a bit restricted with the hood up and the perspex rear window soon went opaque. I tried fitting an external mirror, a nice fancy streamlined racing mirror, but after some moron had wrenched it off and stolen it I went off external mirrors. Did I say the European scene was changing? When the rear perspex panel became too opaque to see through I cut a large hole in it and vision was perfect for the rare occasions I had the hood up, and surprisingly little rain came in. Eventually I began to look upon the open roadster as a motorcycle, and dressed for the part and sat it out even in heavy rain. Providing you did not have to stop it was remarkably good, especially with the passenger seat covered by my special tonneau cover.

The author's 4.2 litre roadster showing the tonneau cover with central zip-fastened joint, made to special order by Robert Betteridge & Co. Ltd.

During the first week of ownership I gave the car its delivery service, with an oil change, and went over everything with my tool kit, tightening the head down and tweaking up all the nuts and bolts, all of which I had to do in a friendly hotel car park, as I did not have time to search out Jaguar agents or suitable garages, on my way to Madrid. There were numerous satisfying differences on the Series 2 cars, introduced at the London Motor Show of 1968, such as the elimination of the separate water header tank for the cooling system, which inevitably rusted through, the change over to Lockheed-Girling brake calipers which were much less corrosion-prone and with better pad retention, different switches on the instrument panel and the elimination of the headlamp covers so that the full 75 watts of each lamp hit the road. The world was beginning to look after our safety by this time, and head-restraints had sprouted out of the backs of the seats, but I took these off the day I got the car and threw them over the hedge. I even received an irate letter from someone who considered I was a social liability, driving about in an open car! Did I say the seventies were going to be sordid?

By the time I was on my way back from Sicily I had done sufficient running-in to let things fly, and the roadster pulled 5000 rpm in top with the hood down. This was quite a lot down on the coupé's maximum on the same stretch of road, but it was to be expected for the Series 2 had the same power output. The shape had changed quite a lot, much of it for the worse. Jaguar had been pressurised by American rules and regulations, the headlamps were no longer faired in, but sat out in the open like two wind-breaks, and the opening in the front of the bonnet was larger to assist the revised cooling system. Add to this the drag of the open two-seater body compared to the smooth

lines of the coupé, and it was no suprise that BJD147H was a good 10 mph slower than FPL660C. From a purely personal point of view I found that 90–95 mph was the comfortable cruising speed, with the hood up or down, due to the increase of wind noise, for although the hood fitted pretty well and was remarkably rigid, its shape generated a lot of wind noise. This diminution in cruising speed was a purely personal fad, in order to avoid fatigue when putting 500 miles into a day's motoring. If you were in a hurry you could cover the ground as easily as in the coupé,

In very hot Southern Italian sunshine, on the way to Sicily, the author looks as though he has been caught in the act of stealing something from the unattended 4.2 litre roadster

and on the infamous Modena–Milan run, from Autostrada gate to Autostrada gate, I improved my best time to 59 minutes in the roadster, with the hood up.

That first trip saw just over 7000 miles clocked up without the slightest trouble, and being short of time I put the car into a London Jaguar agents for a service—oil change in the engine, gearbox and rear axle and a grease all round. Shortly after this there was a strange noise from the rear axle and a bit of a jerk as if the differential wanted to lock up solid. This soon developed into an awful creaking and groaning from the axle when going round slow corners. I feared the worst. However, when I did a bit of cross-checking and research I discovered that the garage had refilled the axle with normal oil, and not the special LS oil recommended for the Salisbury Powr-Lok limited-slip differential. I drained the oil out and refilled with the correct type of lubricant (actually Shell

The author's 1970 roadster photographed by the finishing line of the Montseny mountain hillclimb in Spain on the way to the Spanish Grand Prix in Barcelona

LS) and all was well. The noises disappeared instantly and the axle is still in the car to this day. It was not the fault of the garage, for by now, in fact from September 1967 production, Jaguar had stopped fitting it as standard and only supplied it to special order. They had tried to persuade me that it was not necessary, but knowing my penchant for mountain hairpins and giving it a bootful I was all for having the limited-slip diff. It is in effect a multi-plate clutch within the differential unit lubricated by the axle oil. This is why it has to be special oil and the noises I was getting were the plates protesting at having the wrong kind between them. Naturally the garage had assumed that my roadster was a standard production model, and had put in the standard recommended oil.

Apart from routine changes of consumable items, such as plugs, points, brake pads and tyres, I had a completely trouble-free season of nearly

The much-travelled 4.2 litre E type poses in front of giant concrete podium in the Nüremburg stadium where Hitler held his Third Reich rallies. Today the road in front of it forms the starting area for the Norisring circuit which runs around the stadium

The result of following too closely behind a circus elephant! The crumpled front of the E type roadster on it's return to England after a small contretemps in central France. Luckily the crushed bodywork did not affect any of the mechanical components

25,000 miles, the open-air aspect of the roadster being a pleasant change, but at other times it was a real pain. I became very adept at sky-watching to avoid rain-belts and spent far too much time putting the hood up and down, which in itself was no great hardship, but time-consuming during a twelve-hour day of motoring, mainly because you broke the rhythm of driving, and had to re-overtake much of the traffic you had just passed. From the point of view of exploring alternative routes to avoid black-spots it was a great success, especially over the Alps where you could really enjoy the scenery, as on a motorcycle. You could never do *that* in a GT coupé. If I did get stuck in a traffic snarl-up it was rather pleasant to sit in the sun and read a magazine while people all around me in closed cars overheated and hung out of the windows.

By now the world was well into the safety-era and the E type's classic eared hub nuts were considered to be dangerous, so Jaguar had designed a centre-lock nut without ears for the wire-spoke wheels, fitting them from January 1969 production. In the tool-kit was a heavy bronze forging which fitted over the nut on a self-locking taper, and you hit the ears on this with the wheel hammer. If you lost that special bronze forging I cannot imagine how you would ever get the wheels off. It was all pretty clever, but rather tiresome, and I think it was the Germans who first decided some years earlier that the classic 'ears' were dangerous and might damage a pedestrian! With all that torque from the six-cylinder engine going through the rear hubs I did find a tendency for the nuts to loosen, so that periodic checking and tightening was a good precautionary measure. With the really powerful disc brakes all four hub-splines had a pretty hard life and over the years I found that the hubs could jam badly on the splines if they were not kept well greased, especially if you motored a lot in bad weather conditions and on dusty and muddy surfaces. This I tended to do in the mountains of Italy and Sicily.

Just before the end of the first year with the roadster the alternator gave a scream of agony and then went quiet, but continued to charge healthily and I never did find out what caused it. It was some two years later that it gave up working. That first year ended on a very personal high note, quite unrehearsed and rather satisfying. I was born at the end of 1920, so that the end of 1970 saw me reaching the age of 'half-a-hundred', which by any standards was worth celebrating. I had thoughts of planning for it, but life was so full that it was forgotten. In December I went on a trip to Germany, to visit Mercedes-Benz and Porsche, and to a test-day at the Hockenheimring. The weather was superb—I was happily motoring with the hood down and enjoying the winter sunshine. On the Autobahn south of Frankfurt, ambling along in the eighties a German registered Daimler came up behind me, travelling fast. This was a Jaguar XJ6 with a Daimler radiator grille, called a Daimler Sovereign, and I recognized the driver as one of the Porsche racing team. It was obvious he was on his way to Hockenheim so I tucked in behind him and we had a superb run in close company at 100–110 mph. In the course of it I was reflecting on how pleasant life was when I realized that not only was it my birthday, but it was my 'half-a-hundred' birthday. Just for the hell of it I flattened the accelerator pedal of the E type and wafted by the Daimler, up to my 135 mph terminal speed, before settling down again to my normal gait, thinking 'Happy Birthday'. Later I was talking to the German racing driver and asked why he had a Daimler; he explained that he really wanted a Jaguar, but there was too much delay on delivery, whereas he could have a Daimler version instantly. He found it amusing that people did not expect a Daimler to go fast, not knowing it was really a Jaguar XJ6 suffering from 'badge engineering'. He also found the police took far less interest in it than if it had been a Jaguar.

Chapter 6
5.3, bigger but better?

The white roadster went on and on, just as the red coupé had done, but with it I suffered my only Jaguar accident, entirely due to my own fault. I was creeping through a small French town in heavy traffic, sitting in the hot sunshine and not paying attention, when a lorry in front of me stopped and at 5 mph I drove under the back of it. The bonnet and the right-hand headlamp were severely crushed, but otherwise no damage was done. The car was quite drivable, so I finished the rest of that particular European tour with a very twisted front, which I could not see from the driving seat though everybody else could see it clearly. I had a lot of fun answering the obvious silly question with the equally silly answer about having followed a circus through a French village and at the back was a large elephant. Inadvertently the long protruding nose of the E type just nudged the elephant in a back leg, behind the knee, and I had not realized that this was the trainer's signal for the creature to sit down! A lot of people really believed that story, for they would never have believed I had driven under the back of a stationary lorry.

Back home I gave the car to a London Jaguar

The end of the 6 cylinder E type. A Series Three 4.2 litre roadster that was superseded by the V12 engined model

agent to have a new bonnet fitted, and when it came back they had managed to fit the centre portion of the front bumper upside down, so that the Jaguar emblem was standing on its head. It stayed that way as a shining example of good British workmanship and inspection. It was not long before the paint began to flake off this new bonnet and it was quite obvious that it was from old stock that was well rusted over before being painted. It got so bad that I eventually had to go back to the factory for another one, it was all a sad indication that standards in Britain were falling fast.

During 1971 the Series 3 E type was announced. This was the new V12, and a visit to the factory made it quite clear that there was something new and interesting on the way. The beautiful 5.3-litre V12 engine was beginning to be mass-produced in the old Daimler factory to a degree that was easily going to outpace E type sales, and as we now know all this was the prelude to the V12 saloons and then the XJ-S. The Series 3 E type was little more than a production test-bed to get the new engine under way. After twenty-three years the classic six-cylinder XK engine was being superseded in the E type by an even better unit. I say superseded, cautiously, for the six-cylinder engine was not being abandoned, far from it, for it was still being improved and refined in many small ways.

At the end of 1971 I had a most enjoyable week in Scotland with a Series 3 E type coupé, with a view to changing the 4.2-litre roadster for a V12. For all normal motoring purposes I could not see that the V12 engine gave any particular advantage over the six-cylinder, apart from incredible smoothness and flexibility. Obviously it had a lot more power, and it did everything the 4.2 did but at 20 mph higher speed. Where the 4.2 would cruise at 100 mph with little or no throttle opening, the V12 cruised at 120 mph with the foot eased right back, but at the expense of 15 mpg against 21 mpg. The acceleration of the 4.2 at 100 mph, for instant overtaking or getting ahead of an impending situation, was repeated by the V12 at 120 mph though maximum speed was no better than the 3.8-litre E type. My eyesight, judgement and reflexes could not really cope with these increased speeds as a continual way of motoring. I could

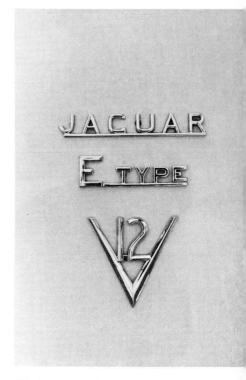

The legend on the luggage compartment lid told it all

see no justification for a V12 for my purposes, even forgetting laws and restrictions that were gathering fast in all directions.

When driven spiritedly, the Series 3 began to show up a lot of short-comings, even though it had been improved with a wider track to match the 8 ft 9 in. wheelbase of the old 2+2. It had lower-profile tyres on wider rims, better brakes with ventilated discs and better shock-absorbers, but even so the new V12 engine was such a big stride forward that the concept of the E type could not keep pace with it, and it was all too easy to run out of road-holding, steering and braking ability if you gave the 5.3 litres their freedom. The days of the E type were numbered and Jaguar were working on a

Above The 'birdcage' grille in the front of the production Series Three Jaguar E type V12, with extra air intake underneath

Left An early V12 E type tried out in the Warwickshire lanes by the author. The wheel arches now have flares, bolt-on steel wheels are now standard, an extra air-scoop under the main radiator opening has been added, but the grille has yet to appear

111

The Series Three in 2+2 form. Still a sleek car, but beginning to look too long for its width. The ratio of width to length is all-important in the aesthetics of styling

replacement that would move them out of the sphere of sports car or GT cars, into a whole new world of luxury high-speed motoring, even accepting that legislation was fast outlawing high speed.

The signs of the future for Jaguar were made clear to me when I was able to borrow an XJ12, a development of the XJ6 saloon powered by a V12 engine. This was in the autumn of 1972 and it proved to be a giant of a car, with road holding and handling up to using the full potential of the V12 engine. I soon realized that the E type era was over, for on a cross-country run you would have been hard pressed to have kept that big saloon in sight with an E type. Eventually, in 1976 the XJ-S

coupé was announced, a car that was clearly designed and developed around the V12 engine, but by the time it appeared my life-style had changed and Europe was no longer the happy care-free motoring paradise it had been in the nineteen-fifties and nineteen-sixties. I felt the world had caught up with me, so I went away and did other things rather than fight against what I did not enjoy.

Production of the Series 3 E type, in 2+2 and roadster form, was gradually run down, and the last fifty to be made were annointed with collector's tags in the form of commemorative plates on the instrument panel. The very last E type of all left the production line in 1975 and was retained

The Series Three E type V12 in roadster form with detachable hardtop. Compared to the original roadster the car has lost its elegant sporting look and Jaguar enthusiasts knew that a replacement had to be nigh

The Series Three 2+2 coupé took the original styling of the E type just too far to be a classical shape. The pressed-steel wheels did little to enhance the Jaguar image of 'Grace . . . Space . . . Pace'

by the factory for sentimental and publicity reasons. Many of us have had the unique opportunity of a drive in this car (HDU555N), the very last E type to be made at the Jaguar factory in Coventry. It was a black roadster.

The last years of my Jaguar motoring tended to dwindle quietly away and as the white roadster approached the 60,000 mile mark I had the only

serious Jaguar breakdown during ten years with
E types. In the middle of France there was a
sudden bang and the clutch pedal went down to
the floor boards. Lying underneath I found some
bits of toggle mechanism in the road and a hole in
the bell-housing, so it was clear what had happened. One of the clutch operating arms had broken
and come out through the bottom of the clutch

A favourite posture for Jaguars used by the firm's publicity department. The Series Three in open roadster and coupé form, both on the long wheelbase

housing. Luckily the hole was not in a vital place so the car was drivable, but the clutch was locked solid with no way of freeing it. I was in the middle of nowhere on one of my back-routes on yellow roads, heading for Le Touquet and the Air Ferry, so I decided to give it a go. With the Jaguar pre-engaged starter motor it was a simple matter to put the gear-lever in first and drive off on the starter motor until the engine fired, which it did within a turn or two. After that it was a case of changing gear without the clutch, which called for some delicate feel and judgement, but after a while I became quite adept at it. The particular route I was following was not a very fast one, but it avoided all towns and sizeable villages, though

The Series Three roadster with V12 engine, wide tyres, wheel-arch flares and deeper tail was beginning to look matronly by the end of the E type life span

there were some major trunk roads to cross. It was beautiful summer weather, I had time on my side so I carried on with the hood down, even managing to stop the night at an hotel and park in the car park, all without a clutch. It meant an enormous amount of stopping and starting the engine and the starter motor stood up to it all magnificently, as did the gearbox. As an exercise in anticipation it was a real challenge. I managed the journey of 375 miles to Le Touquet without drama, though I upset some other motorists when I slowed down long before cross-roads in order to judge my arrival at a gap in the traffic. The essence of the exercise was not to stop at all costs and to free-wheel to rest if it was imperative. Then

Signs of changing times. Enormous rubber over-riders on a V12 Series Three roadster and an air-disturbing outside mirror. The chrome wire-wheels were an 'extra' guaranteed to crack round the spoke nipples if used hard and uncompromisingly

I had to switch off, engage first gear and drive off on the starter motor, the fabulous XK engine firing straight away at 300–400 rpm. I coasted into Le Touquet airport and we pushed the car onto the Air Ferry (of blessed memory and now long gone). At Southend Airport it was pouring with rain and was dark, so at that point I chickened-out and called for help in the form of a trailer, as I could not envisage crossing London without a clutch.

That was the only occasion in more than 200,000 miles of E type motoring that I was unable to reach base under my own steam, and to me that is overall reliability. Jaguars may have had their short-comings and small things may have gone

Left *A standard V12 Series Three roadster. Compare this to a 1961 car and you see the results of 11 years of development of a theme that was exactly right on it's introduction*

This bizarre looking monster is actually a V12 Series Three roadster modified to American national racing rules, competing in the United States

wrong, but their record for keeping going, in sympathetic hands, was remarkable.

The clutch trouble meant a pretty major re-build, with engine and gearbox out but the car was soon back in service and carried on to 106,000 miles before it was pensioned off. In its twilight years it was loaned an experimental six cylinder engine of the type being developed for the XJ6. Outwardly it was a normal XK engine, but much of the engineering inside has been changed to improve production and longevity, for Jaguar engineers were, and still are, always looking for improved materials and methods for the produc-tion engines.

In its final years of useful life I used it to tow a small trailer carrying a racing motorcycle, and for this purpose it was superb. It was a very special trailer with a low centre of gravity and independent suspension by swing-axles with built-in negative camber, so that it would corner as well as the E type. The whole plot would waft up to 80 mph before you realized it, and you could drive about as if the trailer was not there, except

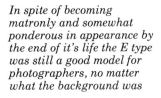

In spite of becoming matronly and somewhat ponderous in appearance by the end of it's life the E type was still a good model for photographers, no matter what the background was

that you needed extra mirrors and a continual searching eye for the law enforcement officers. As I have said already, the world was closing in.

As I ride past a queue of stationary traffic on my BMW motorcycle I notice XJ-S coupés sitting among all the Euroboxes and the hatchback Volkswagen GTIs, and think back fondly to my Jaguar days. They were good days, but life is ever changing and nothing goes on for ever. When an XJ-S wafts past me on the Autoroute I know that I can probably talk myself out of 80 mph on a

End of the line. The very last Series Three E type V12 leaving the assembly line at Browns Lane in 1975. This car HDU555N was retained by the Jaguar factory and still makes public appearances to commemorate the end of an era. The production line restarted with the XJ-S coupé, an entirely different concept of motoring

123

The span of Jaguar sports cars is illustrated by the XK120 roadster of 1953 and the last E type before it received its registration plates. With the cars are members of the management who were in charge after the retirement of Sir William Lyons. On the extreme right is Geoffrey Robinson who was the managing director of Jaguar Cars Ltd for a short time

motorcycle through a radar trap, but it is going to cost the XJ-S driver a lot of money and aggravation if he is caught at 130 mph. Anyway I find 80 mph cruising on a motorcycle gives me the same satisfaction that I used to get at 100 mph in the E type, though I cannot cover the same sort of distances.

Not all Jaguar cars have had classic status, but nobody will dispute the E type being a classic. When it appeared in 1961 it set new standards in motoring, and its performance is still a yardstick today. In its 14-year production run it maintained its looks from start to finish, which says everything for the design team that created the greatest Jaguar of all time.

Specifications

Jaguar E type home market modifications

This listing entitled '*Modifications to home market "E" Types period 1961–1970*' was published by Jaguar Cars but has been rarely seen. Here it is published in full and unaltered.

Major Modifications

1961

> *Introduction of 3.8-litre E Types Open and Fixed Head Coupé Models.* [Geneva Show].

1. Front wheel hubs—introduction of water deflector shields.
2. Self-adjusting handbrake introduced.

1962

1. Footwells introduced and seats positioned further back—to improve leg room.
2. Introduction of Mintex M 33 brake pads.

1963

1. Universal joint shields fitted to rear suspension
2. Thicker ($\frac{1}{2}''$) discs fitted to rear brakes.
3. Axle ratio changed from 3.31:1 to 3.07:1, later changed back to 3.31:1.

1964

> *Introduction of 4.2-litre E types—October 1964.*

1. Diaphragm spring clutch introduced.
2. Dynamo replaced by alternator.
3. New improved radiator fitted.
4. All synchro-mesh gearbox, with 3.07:1 axle ratio.
5. Aluminised exhaust silencers.
6. One piece inlet manifold incorporating water rail.
7. Front and rear hydraulic brake circuits divided using suspended vacuum tandem servo.
8. Dirt shields fitted to front discs.

1965
1. SP41 HR radial tyres fitted.
2. Improved water proofing of distributor cap.

1966
   March 7th—Introduction of 2+2 E type
1. Wide ratio gearbox adopted for Fixed Head Coupé as well as 2+2.

1967
1. Headlamp covers removed.
2. Wide ratio gearbox fitted to Open 2-seater.

1968
   Series 2 E types introduced in October
1. Screen rake revised on 2+2—styling.
2. A 68% increase in air intake aperture.
3. Headlamps brought forward.
4. New enlarged flasher indicators and brake lights.
5. Twin reversing lights positioned immediately inside over-riders.
6. Wrap round bumpers.
7. Twin cooling fans (electric) introduced.
8. New vertical flow radiator with expansion tank.
9. Revision to water pump pulley to improve flow.
10. Revised facia with rocker type switches and improved choke and heater controls.

1969/70
1. New cam shafts for quieter running and longer periods between tappet adjustment.
2. Ballast resister ignition system for improved spark and better cold starting.
3. Steering column lock fitted.

[*1971* Series 3 E type announced at New York Show in March].

Minor Modifications

1961
1. Heated backlight optional on Fixed Head Coupé.
2. New bonnet catches situated inside the car.

1962
1. Brake pedal angle altered.

1963
1. Glove box added between front seats.
2. M 33 brake pads replaced by M 59.
3. Introduction of SP41 radial ply tyres.
4. Modified and improved exhaust system.

1964
1. Covers fitted over boot hinges on Fixed Head Coupé.
2. Boot on Open E type made lockable.
3. Improved petrol pump.

1965
1. Improved screen washer.

1966
1. Clutch pedal angle revised.

1967
1. New plastic-type material replaced canvas on Open E type hoods.

1968
1. Wire-wheel hubs and spokes modified to reduce possibility of spoke breakage.

1969/70
1. All wire-wheeled cars fitted with non-eared hub caps.
2. Introduction of optional (at extra cost) disc wheels.
3. Introduction of gas filled bonnet stay.
4. Revised seat back rests with aperture for fitment of head rests.
5. Arm rest on doors.
6. Car battery powered clock.

Jaguar E type production

Model	Body style	Engine	Production run	Number made
Series 1	Open two seater	3.8-litre	Mar. 1961–Oct. 1964	7827
	Fixed-head coupé	3.8-litre	Mar. 1961–Oct. 1964	7669
	Open two-seater	4.2-litre	Oct. 1964–Sept. 1968	9548
	Fixed-head coupé	4.2-litre	Oct. 1964–Sept. 1968	7770
	2+2 fixed-head	4.2-litre	Mar. 1966–Sept. 1968	5598
Series 2	Open two-seater	4.2-litre	Oct. 1968–Sept. 1970	8627
	Fixed-head coupé	4.2-litre	Oct. 1968–Sept. 1970	4855
	2+2 fixed-head	4.2-litre	Oct. 1968–Sept. 1970	5326
Series 3	Open two-seater	5.3-litre V12	Apr. 1971–Feb. 1975	7990
	2+2 fixed-head	5.3-litre V12	Apr. 1971–Sept. 1973	7297
			Total	72507

NB—The above information is based on that in *Jaguar Sports Cars* by Paul Skilleter in which the author notes the following: 'Production figures have been calculated from factory listings of chassis numbers but should be regarded as a guide only, within the limits of several units either way for the various totals'.

Specifications

Engine	3.8-litre	4.2-litre	5.3-litre
No. of cylinders	six	six	twelve
Formation	in-line	in-line	vee
Bore	87 mm (3.42 in.)	92.07 mm (3.625 in.)	90 mm (3.54 in.)
Stroke	106 mm (4.17 in.)	106 mm (4.17 in.)	70 mm (2.75 in.)
Capacity	3781 cc	4235 cc	5343 cc
Camshafts	2 OHC	2 OHC	One per bank
Comp. ratio	9:1	9:1	9:1
Carburettors	SU HD8	SU HD8	Zenith Strom. 175CDSE
Max. power	265 bhp (SAE)	265 bhp (SAE)	314 bhp (SAE)
Rpm	5500	5400	6200
Max. torque	260 lb. ft.	283 lb. ft.	349 lb. ft.
Rpm	4000	4000	3600
Ign. timing	10° btdc		
Points gap	0.014–.016 in.		
Valve timing	IO 15° btdc	as 3.8 litre	IO 17° btdc
	IC 57° abdc		IC 59° abdc
	EO 57° bbdc		EO 59° bbdc
	EC 15° atdc		EC 17° atdc
	Overlap 30°		Overlap 30°

Tappets	IN 0.004 in.		
	EX 0.006 in.	as 3.8 litre	
Battery	12 v 57 amp hr		12 v 60 amp hr
Fuel tank	14 gal		18 gal
Headlamps	60/60 watt	75/60 watt	75/60 watt
Transmission	4 sp. & rev.	4 sp. & rev. (Auto optional)	4 sp. & rev. (Auto optional)
Ratios 1st	11.18:1	8.23:1	9.00:1
2nd	6.16:1	5.34:1	5.86:1
3rd	4.25:1	3.90:1	4.27:1
4th	3.31:1	3.07:1	3.07:1
Rev.	11.18:1	8.23:1	9.00:1
Alternative axle	2.89:1	2.89:1	3.31:1
ratios	3.07:1	3.27:1	3.54:1
	3.27:1	3.77:1	
	3.77:1	4.09:1	
	4.09:1		

Chassis/body Steel monocoque with tubular sub-frame to carry front suspension and engine/gearbox unit common to all models.

Wheelbase	2438 mm (8 ft 0 in.)	2438 mm (8 ft 0 in.) (2+2) 2667 mm (8 ft 9 in.)	2667 mm (8 ft 9 in.)
Track (front)	1269 mm (4 ft 2 in.)	1269 mm (4 ft 2 in.)	1371 mm (4 ft 6½ in.)
(rear)	1269 mm (4 ft 2 in.)	1269 mm (4 ft 2 in.)	1346 mm (4 ft 5 in.)
Overall length	4457 mm (14 ft 7½ in.)	4457 mm (14 ft 7½ in.) (2+2) 4673 mm (15 ft 4 in.)	4673 mm (15 ft 4 in.)
Overall width	1631 mm (5 ft 4¼ in.)	1656 mm (5 ft 5¼ in.)	1681 mm (5 ft 6¼ in.)
Weight Open	2688 lb	2800 lb	3226 lb
Coupé	2670 lb	2811 lb	
2+2		3102 lb	3304 lb
Brakes (front)	11 in.	11 in.	11 in. (ventilated)
(rear)	10 in.	10 in.	10 in.
Wheels	15 in. 5K	15 in. 5K	15 in. 6K
Tyres	6.40×15	6.40×15	E70VR×15

Steering   Rack and pinion, common to all models.

Suspension (front): Independent by wishbones, longitudinal torsion bars, common to all models   telescopic shock absorbers and anti-roll torsion bar.

(rear):   Independent by lower transverse tubular link, forward facing radius arm, universally jointed drive shaft provides lateral location. Twin coil spring/shock absorber units each side. Anti-roll torsion bar.

Performance

Max. speed mph (claimed)	150 coupé 149 open	150 coupé 136 2+2 140 open	142 2+2 146 open
Acceleration 0–100 mph in seconds	16.2	17.2	15.4
Fuel consumption mpg	18–20	18	15

Suppliers of parts for the Jaguar E type

Engine

Cylinder block casting (iron)—Leyland Motors Ltd., Leyland, Lancs.

Cylinder head casting (alloy)—West Yorkshire Foundries, Leeds, Yorks. William Mills, Wednesbury, Staffs.

Crankshaft—Smith-Clayton Forge Ltd., Lincoln. Scottish Stamping & Eng. Co. Ltd., Ayr, Scotland.

Crankshaft damper—Metalastik, Leicester.

Connecting rods—Forging & Presswork Ltd., Birmingham. Albion Drop Forgings Ltd., Coventry. Bretts Stamping Co., Coventry.

Connecting rod bolts—Garringtons Ltd., Bromsgrove, Worcester. Acton Bolts Ltd., London.

Pistons—British Piston Ring Co. Ltd., Coventry.

Valves—Valves Ltd., Coventry.

Valve guides, seats, tappets—British Piston Ring Co. Ltd., Coventry.

Gaskets—Coopers Mechanical Joints Ltd., Slough, Bucks.

Aluminium castings and clutch housing—Dialoy Ltd., Cardiff. West Yorkshire Foundries, Leeds, Yorks.

Sump—William Mills, Wednesbury, Staffs.

Bearings (plain)—Vandervell Products Ltd., Acton, London.

Timing chain—Renold Chain Ltd., Manchester. Coventry Chain Ltd., Manchester.

Oil pump—Hobourn Eaton Manufacturing Co., Strood, Kent.

Water pump casting—West Yorkshire Foundries, Leeds, Yorks. Qualcast Ltd., Derby.

Water pump seal—Morgan Crucible Co. Ltd., London

Flywheel—Garringtons Ltd., Bromsgrove, Worcester.
  Clydesdale Stampings Ltd., Dudley, Worcs.
Clutch—Borg & Beck Co. Ltd., Leamington Spa.
Engine mountings—Metalastic, Leicester.
Clutch linings—Ferodo Ltd., Chapel-en-le-Frith,
  Stockport.

Transmission and suspension Gearbox casting—Dartmouth Auto Castings, Smethwick.
  Qualcast Ltd., Derby.
Bearings—Hoffman Manufacturing Co. Ltd., Chelmsford,
  Essex.
Gear stampings—English Steel Co., Sheffield.
Propeller shaft—Hardy Spicer & Co. Ltd., Birmingham.
Half shafts—Hardy Spicer & Co. Ltd., Birmingham.
Axle (rear)—Salisbury Transmission Co. Ltd.,
  Birmingham.
Hubs—Alford & Alder Ltd., Hemel Hempstead, Herts.
Bearings—British Timken Ltd., Northampton.
Front suspension—Alford & Alder Ltd., Hemel
  Hempstead, Herts.
Torsion bars—English Steel Corp. Ltd., Birmingham.
Shock absorbers—Girling Ltd., Birmingham.

Brakes Calipers—Dunlop Rubber Co. Ltd., Coventry. Lockheed
  AP, Leamington Spa.
Pipes—British Bundy Tubing, London.
Friction pads—British Belting & Asbestos Ltd., (Mintex)
  Birmingham.

Wheels and Tyres Dunlop Rubber Co. Ltd., Coventry.

Bodywork Frame tubes—Reynold Tube Co. Ltd., Birmingham.
Bonnet panels—Abbey Panel & Sheet Metal Co. Ltd.,
Coventry.
Wiring harness—Joseph Lucas Ltd., Birmingham.
Ignition, lamps, fuel pump, battery—Joseph Lucas Ltd.,
  Birmingham.
Instruments—Smiths Motor Accessories Ltd., London
Body accessories—Wilmot Breedon Ltd., Birmingham.

Miscellaneous Leather—Connollys Bros. Ltd., London.
Radiator—Marston Excelsior Ltd., Leeds.
Water hoses—John Bull Rubber Co. Ltd., Leicester. Avon
  India Rubber Co. Ltd., Melksham, Wilts. Alfred Roberts
  Ltd., Birmingham.
Glass—Triplex Safety Glass Co. Ltd., London.

The men behind the Jaguar E type

Sir William Lyons
Bill Heynes
Claude Baily
Wally Hassan
Harry Mundy
Malcom Sayer
Phil Weaver
Harry Weslake

Bibliography on the Jaguar E type

Jaguar Sports Cars by Paul Skilleter—G. T. Foulis, 1975
Jaguar E-type—A Collectors Guide by Paul Skilleter—Motor Racing Publications, 1971
E-type—End of an Era by Chris Harvey—The Oxford Illustrated Press, 1977
Jaguars in Competition by Chris Harvey—Osprey Publishing Ltd., 1979
Jaguar. The history of a great British Car by Andrew Whyte—Patrick Stephens Ltd., 1980

Acknowledgements

No one can deny that the history of the Jaguar E type is not well recorded between hard covers— look at the essential bibliography earlier. Denis Jenkinson has added his personal experiences of the cars to produce this worthy addition. Gathering illustrative material when the aim is to offer previously unseen material is therefore extremely difficult.

Our thanks must go first to the author himself. Jenks has kindly loaned many photographs from his personal collection. Others who have helped greatly are as follows, in alphabetical order: *Autocar*, British Leyland and Jaguar Cars both together and separately, Mike Cook of BL's American operation, Mirco Decet, William Goodall of Newlands Motors, LAT, Motor Racing Graphics, the National Motor Museum, Paul Skilleter and Andrew Whyte. Peter Coltrin supplied some of the shots loaned by Jenks.

Further special thanks go to Ray Hutton, editor of *Autocar* and Tony Curtis, editor of *Motor*, for their kind permissions to allow us to reproduce their famous 'road test results pages' of the first Jaguar E type.

Index

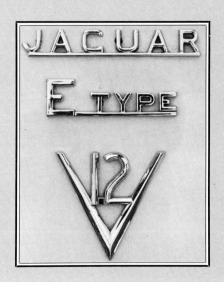